Healing through Relating

A Skill-Building Book for Therapists

Jon Frederickson, MSW

Seven Leaves Press

Seven Leaves Press
www.sevenleavespress.com

Ordering Information

Quantity sales. Special discounts are available on quantity purchases by corporations, associations, and others. For details, contact the "Special Sales Department" at the address above.

Orders by US trade bookstores and wholesalers. Please contact BCH: (800) 431-1579 or visit www.bookch.com for details.

Printed in the United States of America

Cataloging-in-Publication data

Names: Frederickson, Jon, author.
Title: Healing through relating : a skill-building book for therapists / Jon Frederickson, MSW.
Description: Includes bibliographical references and index. | Kensington, MD: Seven Leaves Press, 2023.
Identifiers: LCCN: | ISBN: 978-0-9883788-2-7 (paperback) | ISBN 978-0-9883788-3-4 (ebook)
Subjects: LCSH Cognitive therapy. | Psychotherapist and patient. | Interpersonal relations. |
    Interpersonal communication. | Communication--Psychological aspects. | Psychotherapists--Training of.
    | BISAC PSYCHOLOGY / Psychotherapy / Counseling | PSYCHOLOGY / Education & Training
Classification: LCC RC480.8 .F74 2023 | DDC 616.89/14--dc23

First Edition

27 26 25 24 23   1 2 3 4 5 6 7 8 9 10

PRAISE FOR *HEALING THROUGH RELATING*

"Master therapist and award-winning author Jon Frederickson provides therapists with a clear, accessible, and highly effective path to clinical skill development. Along with over forty skill-building exercises, the book contains advice for cultivating motivation to practice, transtheoretical principles for effective therapy, and other guidance that will be helpful for trainees. This book is a special opportunity to learn from a master teacher!"

> —Tony Rousmaniere, PsyD, Executive Director, Sentio Counseling Center, President-Elect, Division 39 of the American Psychological Association, and coauthor of the Essentials of Deliberate Practice series

"Frederickson provides skill-building exercises, instruction in how to conduct them, and video and audio resources. But as important is his conceptual framework that includes six categories of skills necessary for effective working alliances. By addressing skill categories that others have not covered in their DP books, manuals, or platforms, Frederickson makes a unique contribution to the training literature."

> —Rodney Goodyear, PhD, Program Coordinator, Masters of Counseling and Psychotherapy, University of Redlands, and Emeritus Professor of Counseling Psychology, University of Southern California

"If you learn to play an instrument very well, your 'technique' can become a prison. But if you step outside the technique and into the unfolding musical conversation of therapy—as Jon Frederickson shows us—a deeper relationship awaits."

> —Daryl Chow, PhD, blogger at *Frontiers of Psychotherapist Development* and author of *The First Kiss: Undoing the Intake Model and Igniting the First Sessions in Psychotherapy*

"Frederickson is a master at transforming core therapeutic principles into clear exercises that help therapists develop a broad repertoire of advanced skills. These skills will help therapists of any orientation flexibly match interventions to patients' specific needs in the moment, leading to improved outcomes."

> —Peter Lilliengren, PhD, Assistant Professor, Department of Psychology, Stockholm University, Sweden

"All my students are recognizing just how important—in fact, crucial—skill-building exercises are. Even though they were anxious about them or a little resistant early on, they are a game changer in seeing therapists' skills develop."

> —Angela Cooper, PhD, Assistant Professor, Department of Psychiatry, Dalhousie Medical School

"I use Jon's skill-building exercises with undergraduate counseling students and graduate students in clinical psychology. The opportunity to learn and practice these skills is consistently ranked as one of the most effective aspects of my courses and supervision. More advanced psychotherapy supervisees have reported that the skill-building practice improved their clinical effectiveness and led to personal and professional growth."

—Deborah L. Pollack, PhD, Assistant Professor of Psychology, Utica University, and Clinical Assistant Professor, SUNY Upstate Medical University

"The skill-building exercises accelerated the learning and implementation of an evidence-based practice, improving outcomes with clients, and developing clinicians became appropriately confident about their skills. Having an opportunity to build the capacity to intervene in sessions by practicing these skills *outside* of the therapy session prepares clinicians to respond effectively *in* session."

—Asta Lynch, LCSW, Outpatient Services Bureau Director, Arlington County Community Services Board, Department of Human Services

"The stimulating real-life exercises, accompanied by crystal-clear explanations, helped me integrate important principles of clinical theory and technique at a deep level. They helped my 'attachment-muscle memory' set in so my brain could forget about shoulds and should-nots. I became freer to listen and discover the true art of psychotherapy, see the potential in my patients, and most importantly help them see and feel it. I highly recommend this book."

—Yair Braun, PhD, Center for the Treatment of Eating Disorders, Rambam Medical Center, Israel

"What has had the most impact on me as a CBT therapist is the ability to assess and regulate anxiety. Second is the ability to get a clear focus faster and avoid getting caught in rumination and vague, externalizing conversations. Third, I learned to ask for patients' reactions to me and how they perceive me. It feels great to be able to help patients—I can feel their relief."

—Mattias Boije, Social Worker and Cognitive Behavioral Therapist, Outpatient Psychiatry, Höglandssjukhuset Eksjö, Sweden

"This book is a phenomenal contribution to the field. This is an approach to training that I encourage all new therapists to consider, as well as anyone like me with gaps in our development. The exercises are incredibly valuable to deepen skills or to course-correct."

—Lisa Barker, Clinical Counselor, Vancouver, BC

"As a trainee, I found it difficult to establish the therapeutic task and instead was often caught up in the client's diversifying. Jon's skill-building exercises helped me establish the therapeutic task early on while co-creating a therapeutic alliance."

—Richard Cox, Reg. MBACP, Psychodynamic Counselor and Psychotherapist, Buxton, UK

Contents

Acknowledgments   v

Chapter One: What Makes Therapy Work?   1

Chapter Two: How to Use These Exercises to Become More Skillful   9

Chapter Three: Co-Creating Safety to Make It Safe to Depend   15
Stage One: Regulating Anxiety   16
   Skill-Building Exercise One: Assessing How Anxiety Appears in the Body   16
   Skill-Building Exercise Two: Identifying and Regulating Anxiety   19
   Skill-Building Exercise Three: Regulating Anxiety by Paying Attention to an Anxiety Symptom   23
   Skill-Building Exercise Four: Helping Patients Pay Attention to Rather Than Ignore Anxiety
     So They Can Regulate It   25
   Skill-Building Exercise Five: Blocking Strategies That Prevent Anxiety Regulation and Then
     Regulating Anxiety   29
   Skill-Building Exercise Six: Building the Capacity to Pay Attention to Anxiety   32

Chapter Four: Developing the Right to Depend on Someone   35
Stage Two: Declaring a Problem to Work On   35
   Skill-Building Exercise One: Offering Nonproblems Rather Than Real Problems   36
   Skill-Building Exercise Two: Changing Topics to Avoid Declaring a Problem   42
   Skill-Building Exercise Three: Offering Vague Answers to Avoid Declaring a Problem 44
   Skill-Building Exercise Four: Offering Thoughts Rather Than a Problem to Work On   47
   Skill-Building Exercise Five: Helping Patients Who Say That Someone Else Thinks They
     Should Be in Therapy   49
   Skill-Building Exercise Six: Helping When Patients Ask What They Should Work On   53
   Skill-Building Exercise Seven: Review Exercise   55
   Skill-Building Exercise Eight: Handling Denial of a Problem   58

Chapter Five: Is It Safe to Have a Separate Mind and Will in Therapy?   61
Stage Three: Declaring One's Will to Work on the Problem   61
   Skill-Building Exercise One: Inviting the Experience of Will   62
   Skill-Building Exercise Two: Attributing the Will to Do Therapy on to Others   64
   Skill-Building Exercise Three: Attributing the Will to Do Therapy on to the Therapist   66
   Skill-Building Exercise Four: Deactivating Patients' Defiance   68

Skill-Building Exercise Five: Helping Patients with Anxiety When They Declare Their Will to Do Therapy   71

Skill-Building Exercise Six: Integrative Exercise: Moving from No Alliance to Alliance   73

Stage Four: Mobilizing the Patient's Will to the Task   76

Skill-Building Exercise One: Helping When Patients Attribute Their Will to Others   76

Skill-Building Exercise Two: Mobilizing Patients' Will to Work toward Their Goal   81

Skill-Building Exercise Three: Helping Patients with Defiance   83

Skill-Building Exercise Four: Helping Patients Who Attribute Their Wish to Get Well to the Therapist   85

Skill-Building Exercise Five: Mobilizing Patients' Will by Using Their Words   87

Skill-Building Exercise Six: Responding to Denial through Fantasy I   89

Skill-Building Exercise Seven: Responding to Denial through Fantasy II   90

Skill-Building Exercise Eight: Responding to Denial through Fantasy III   92

Skill-Building Exercise Nine: Responding to Denial through Words   93

Skill-Building Exercise Ten: Dealing with Denial   96

Skill-Building Exercise Eleven: Identifying and Deactivating Misperceptions   97

Skill-Building Exercise Twelve: Working with Patients' Ambivalence   99

Skill-Building Exercise Thirteen: Addressing Passivity   100

Stage Five: Mobilizing the Patient to Work toward a Positive Goal   104

Skill-Building Exercise One: Turning Problems into Positive Goals   104

Skill-Building Exercise Two: Turning Avoidance Strategies into Positive Goals   106

Skill-Building Exercise Three: Turning Negative Goals into Positive Goals for Therapy   107

Skill-Building Exercise Four: Turning a Lack of Capacity into a Positive Goal   109

Skill-Building Exercise Five: Turning Negative Expectations into Realistic Hope   110

Skill-Building Exercise Six: Getting Consensus on What We Do and Why We Do It   112

Chapter Six: How to Prevent Dropouts from Treatment   115

Skill-Building Exercise One: Identifying Warning Signs of Dropout   116

Skill-Building Exercise Two: Learning to Identify Dropout Behavior   119

Skill-Building Exercise Three: Practicing How to Begin Healing Ruptures   120

Chapter Seven: What to Do When You Don't Want to Practice   125

Chapter Eight: Transtheoretical Principles for Effective Therapy   131

Conclusion   133

Teachers' Guide for Using These Exercises in Class   135

Bibliography   139

Index   147

About the Author   151

Acknowledgments

I would like to thank Alexandre Vaz, Diane Byster, Deborah Pollack, Tony Rousmaniere, Mark Karras, and Michelle Salois for their comments on previous drafts of this book. I would also like to thank Tobias Nordqvist, Peter Liliengren, Liv Raissi, Bjarne Thannel, Vesla Birkbak, Jeanne Isaksen, Brian Kok, Lindsay Chipman, Mark Vail, Julie Cochrane, and Beata Zaloga for their suggestions based on using these skill-building studies in their classes. And I would like to thank all the students I have taught who have let me know the skills they needed and what worked and what didn't. Without their advice and feedback, this book could not have been written. A special thank you goes to Alexandre Vaz for co-creating and editing the video demonstrations.

And finally, I would like to thank all the music teachers who taught me through using skill-building exercises known as etude books: Henry Paulisich, Jim Crowder, David Kennedy, Lud Wangberg, Robert Elworthy, Philip Farkas, and Ted Thayer. Their focus on the deliberate practice of specific musical skills through etudes arranged in a progressive order gave me my foundation. I have translated this use of deliberate practice in music to the learning of skills in psychotherapy. But I owe this experiential knowledge to them.

CHAPTER ONE

What Makes Therapy Work?

R esearch has shown that therapy works. But specifically, how does therapy help people change? Some claim that change depends on the treatment model we use. Yet, differences in outcome between treatment models are modest (Benish, Imel, and Wampold 2008; Gerger, Munder, and Barth 2014; Tran and Gregor 2016). Unique methods do not create uniquely better results. Since outcomes are similar, what factors common to most models make therapy effective? Meta-analyses have shown that effective common factors across therapy models include the following:

- A good relationship
- Consensus between patient and therapist on a specific therapeutic task
- Agreement between patient and therapist on a positive goal the patient wants to achieve
- A persuasive reason to do the task to achieve that goal (Wampold and Imel 2015)

According to Norcross and Lambert (2018), the quality of the therapy relationship accounts for client improvement as much as, and probably more than, the specific ingredients of a particular treatment method. Thus, all therapists need relational skills that create an effective alliance to ensure a good outcome (Norcross and Lambert 2018, 8). Those skills include the following:

- Regulating the patient's anxiety so it is safe to declare a problem
- Helping the patient declare a problem
- Helping the patient declare his will to work on his problem
- Helping the patient declare a positive goal to work toward
- Getting consensus on the therapeutic task to achieve the patient's positive goal

All the while, the therapist must support the patient's wish for change while empathizing with his fear of it. Then they can work toward his goal.

Before we can begin therapy in any model, anxiety must be regulated so the patient feels safe. Then there must be a problem for which he wants help. Then we need to find out if he wants to work on that problem. These steps create the preconditions for a therapeutic alliance. Without a problem that he wants to work on to achieve a positive goal, there would be no reason to do therapy.

In a common factors theory (Bailey and Ogles 2019), certain principles of change are present in most effective therapies. These principles can be described and applied flexibly, and they are associated with good outcomes. Each of the skills in this manual follows these basic principles that apply to all effective models of therapy:

- If anxiety is not regulated, the patient cannot feel safe enough to work with you.
- If a patient cannot declare a problem, there is no reason to do therapy.
- If it is not the patient's will to do therapy, we have no right to ask him to do what he does not want to do.
- If there is no positive goal to work toward, therapy can achieve nothing worthwhile from the patient's perspective.
- Without a consensus on how to work on the problem, we cannot work together.

I offer here a metatheory to use for building a therapeutic alliance before you propose your particular model of treatment. These metatheoretical principles for alliance building require common foundational skills. Perhaps the most fundamental principle is that we reinforce change and not the behaviors that prevent it. All therapies reinforce one thing and not another (Lundh 2014). Thus, we must be clear about which patient and therapist behaviors promote change and which do not.

For example, in any effective therapy, patients must face their fears to master them (Lambert 2013). Here, we show how to help patients face the fears that would otherwise prevent them from forming a therapeutic alliance. Perhaps the patient is afraid to declare a problem, his wish to work on it, or a positive goal. We must address all those fears first so that the patient can form a therapeutic alliance.

The goal here is not to follow rules slavishly. That leads to poor outcomes (Vacoch and Strupp 2000). Instead, if we understand the basic principles of relationship building and the skills associated with them, we can apply those principles and skills flexibly to develop a healing relationship.

For an overview of the relational principles that guide all therapies, see HTRBook.com/IntroAV.

WHAT PATIENTS NEED: A GOOD RELATIONSHIP WITH YOU

Ample research shows that the key to a better outcome in therapy is the healing relationship you co-create with your patient, not the treatment model you use (Norcross and Wampold 2019). This makes sense since if "relational damage is the core of trauma, . . . the relationship is the core of healing trauma" (Norcross and Wampold 2019, 4). In other words, what was harmed in a relationship we must heal in this relationship.

Models differ very little regarding patient outcomes (Benish, Imel, and Wampold 2008; Gerger, Munder, and Barth 2014; Tran and Gregor 2016). But therapists differ a lot within each model (Wampold and Imel 2015). For example, patients with the best therapists change ten times faster than the average patient. But patients with the worst therapists get worse (Okiishi et al. 2003). This is not an isolated study (see Baldwin and Imel 2013; Wampold and Brown 2006; Minami et al. 2012; Wampold and Imel 2015).

If your model does not guarantee your effectiveness, what does? Your relational skills as a therapist. And what differentiates the best therapists from the rest? They engage in deliberate practice of relational skills (Chow et al. 2015).

But don't all of us have relational skills? Of course! Everyone knows how to relate to people. That's how children survive: they learn to connect to the people they depend on for their survival. So, the question then becomes, what relational skills did we acquire, and what results do they create?

Securely attached therapists get better alliances and outcomes with more highly impaired and distressed patients (Schauenberg et al. 2010; Strauss and Petrowski 2017). When invited to form a therapeutic alliance, these highly impaired patients present with anxiety and avoidant responses. More securely attached therapists become less anxious and defensive when this occurs, with fewer negative countertransference reactions. To help you be less anxious and defensive with patients, we will examine why patients become anxious and hesitant when starting therapy.

The Universal Relational Problem Patients Present

Every therapy begins with the offer of a healing relationship. We offer a secure attachment (Bowlby 1969) where the patient can safely reveal himself. First, we ask about the problem for which he wants our help. Then we look into his difficulties, their origin, and their history. But what if that is impossible? Some patients may flood with anxiety before they arrive at your office. They might assume you are another abuser and equate you with a perpetrator in their past. We want to co-create a conscious alliance. But the patients' fears created a misalliance. What happened?

He seeks a healing relationship, but past relationships prepared him for pain (Bowlby 1973, 1980). If depending on a parent for help was dangerous, he learned to hide his need so his parent could love him (Bowlby 1969, 1973; Hartmann 1965). We conceal our needs through thought distortions, maladaptive behaviors, defenses, or "security operations" (A. Beck 1967; Freud 1923; Sullivan 1947, 1953). The patient reduced his parents' anxiety to restore security in their insecure relationship by hiding his needs. Unfortunately, if he hid his needs with them, he might hide them with you too.

These responses of anxiety and avoidance strategies in therapy are not wrong. Instead, every response precisely expresses the patient's need at this moment so that we learn where he needs our help. Our task is to discover why his reaction is perfect. If depending makes him anxious, we can regulate his anxiety, so he can feel safe depending on a therapist.

He wants help. But his anxiety signals that seeking help can lead to pain. Thus, he may avoid asking for help by not telling you the problem he wants your help with. When he does not declare a problem, he is not resisting you. Instead, he is collaborating with you *according to the rules of insecure attachments*. He learned that he should hide his need to keep a relationship (Bowlby 1973, 1980; Evans 1996; Sullivan 1953). He fears you cannot love him if he doesn't cover up what cannot be loved: his need for help (Post and Semrad 1965). That's why he avoids declaring a problem, revealing his separate will to get better, or setting a positive goal.

Moving from an Insecure Attachment to a Secure Attachment

Since every therapy model involves a relationship, therapists need to understand what happens when we form one.

With every patient, we find the same pattern:

1. The therapist invites the patient to depend on the therapist.
2. Depending triggers anxiety in the patient, a sign that depending was dangerous.
3. Anxiety mobilizes avoidance strategies that show the therapist how the patient learned to handle that danger in the past to keep a relationship.

When we invite a patient to share a problem, he often hesitates. He isn't afraid to put a problem into words; he is afraid to depend on you. His body speaks to us through its secret, silent, wordless language: anxiety. Anxiety tells us the patient's history: depending was dangerous. His treatment-interfering behaviors—his avoidance strategies—tell us how he dealt with that danger. For instance, he might avoid sharing a problem, change the topic, or become vague. Thus, anxiety and treatment-interfering behaviors are how the past speaks to the present through bodily reactions (anxiety) and automatic avoidance strategies.

Patients who grew up in insecure attachments had to adapt to insecure connections. When caretakers hurt, abandoned, abused, or neglected them, they learned that relationships lead to pain, not help. So, they act accordingly. These automatic relational behaviors of anxiety and hiding their needs were adaptive in their original traumatic relationships. In fact, those behaviors may have saved their lives in the past. But today, these same avoidance behaviors create their problems.

A therapist might mistakenly think that anxiety or avoidance behaviors are obstacles. They aren't. They are the pathway to healing. Anxiety and avoidance strategies show you where the patient needs your help in this moment. *By revealing his insecure attachment behaviors, the patient is already collaborating perfectly in therapy.* Therefore, we must focus on the therapist's relational behaviors.

This book will show you how to regulate anxiety so it is safe for patients to depend upon you. You will learn skills so you can help patients with avoidance patterns they don't see. And you will learn how to invite, promote, and strengthen behaviors that will lead to a healing therapeutic alliance.

MYTHS ABOUT THE THERAPEUTIC RELATIONSHIP

There are many myths about the skills we need to be good therapists. And those myths can prevent us from improving as therapists. Let's examine some of the most common myths about therapy skills.

Myth: A teacher once told me, "All you need is to log enough hours."

Reality: Time doesn't create a good relationship. Two people relating well create a good relationship. It's not the amount of time. Patients can be in therapy for decades but never form a therapeutic alliance. How can this be? For instance, if the patient takes a passive position, therapy reinforces passivity instead of actively working toward a goal. Or if the patient blames others for his problems, he will get better at blaming, not at changing. The more we practice, the better we get. If we practice bad relating, we get better at that. Thus, always ask yourself, "What are we doing with our time in this session?"

Myth: "All you need is good social skills and to be a warm person."

Reality: I was afraid of my first placement in graduate school because I had never worked as a therapist before. When I brought up my concerns to my teacher, she replied, "If your social skills have taken you this far, they'll take you through this." But my social skills didn't tell me how to respond when a schizophrenic patient hallucinated a devil in my office. If social skills were enough, the patient's family and friends would already have healed him. And if social skills were sufficient, all therapists would have excellent outcomes. But we don't. The top 20 percent of therapists are consistently more effective *than the other 80 percent combined* (Miller and Hubble 2011). It's not general social skills but specific therapeutic skills that account for that difference (Norcross and Wampold 2019).

Myth: "The patient didn't want to do therapy."

Reality: Every patient's response shows how *she is already doing therapy*. It's just that the patient might not do therapy the way *you* want. It's not her job to do therapy your way. It's the patient's job to show us how she relates with everyone. But when the patient responds in a way we don't like, we may think she is doing therapy wrong. In fact, she is doing therapy right. She always shows us the precise problems she needs help with. She reveals her implicit relational learning (Lyons-Ruth 1996), how she learned to relate in earlier relationships. For instance, suppose we ask the patient what she wants to work on, and she doesn't tell us. We can get frustrated and mistakenly think that the patient doesn't want to do therapy with us. Instead, she shows us how she learned not to depend on people. *That's* her problem.

We often get frustrated because we are waiting for the patient we want to work with rather than working with the patient we have. When we say that the patient resists therapy, we may be failing to accept the patient the way she is and the responses she asks us to help her with. Completely accept the patient as she is, problems and all.

Myth: "All the patient needs is empathy."
Reality: Does a chef need only salt and pepper? Relating, like cooking, is far more complex. Consider empathy. Empathy for what? Suppose a depressed patient wants to divorce her abusive husband. If you empathize only with her anger toward her husband, she may become excessively anxious. If you empathize only with her wish to divorce, she may focus on her husband's good qualities. If you empathize only with her anxiety, she may remain stuck. Patients need complex empathy with *all* aspects of their conflict, not just simple empathy with one part of it. For instance, the patient might need empathy with her wish to divorce, her fear of doing so, and her ways of avoiding that wish. Only then will she feel more fully heard and understood.

Myth: "This patient is not motivated to do therapy."
Reality: Patients always have multiple motivations. Our job? Figure out what those motivations are. People who are not in conflict don't come to therapy. Every day, seven billion people successfully stay out of therapists' offices. Patients come to you precisely because they are in conflict: they want to change and fear change. They hope you will help them and fear you will hurt them. Thus, patients' motivations often conflict with one another. If the therapist does not see both sides of the patient's conflict, she might claim the patient does not want to do therapy. But that's not true. The therapist sees only the patient's treatment interfering behavior. She does not see the patient's simultaneous desire for and fear of help.

Patients almost always want to do therapy. The problem is that they have a conflict about asking for help. "If I reveal my problems to you, will you judge, hurt, or abandon me?" Patients want a new relationship but fear an old one. They are motivated to do therapy but not to have another bad relationship. Since they may not know how to create a relationship for positive change, they need your help.

Patients do not resist therapy. Nor do they resist you. *Instead, they resist the bad relationship they fear they will have with you.* Therefore, it makes no sense to encourage the patient to have a relationship with you if she fears it will bring pain. That's why we need to sort out the expectations that therapy stirs up. Once the patient relates to you instead of an image of someone else, she can then stop hiding and reveal her desires.

Myth: "If I follow this model of therapy, my patient will get better."
Reality: No therapy model has been proven to be more effective than any other (Norcross and Wampold 2019; Wampold and Imel 2015). Further, ritualistic following of manuals

leads to a worse outcome (Vacoch and Strupp 2000). The best therapists within each model have excellent relational skills that lead to good therapeutic alliances (Tracey et al. 2014). Thus, the quality of the relationship is the most important factor that the therapist can contribute to the effectiveness of therapy.

If you follow a model and forget to build the alliance, you will lose the patient. Models don't heal patients. Relationships do. Since the relational skills of co-creating a therapeutic alliance are so important, this book will not teach rules to follow but principles to apply flexibly.

Myth: "I asked him what his problem was, and he didn't have one. So, this intervention didn't help."

Reality: Sometimes, therapists imagine that you'll get the answer you are looking for if you ask a question once. That is magic. A patient is not a soda machine where you push a button, and a bottle of soda pops out. In therapy, when we ask a question, we may get a wide variety of responses that may not appear to answer the question you asked. Why?

When you inquire about the patient's problem, you invite the patient to depend on you. But if depending led to pain, a patient may become anxious and deny that he has a problem. He will do what he was told to do as a child: "Stop bothering me," "Why are you complaining?" or "Shut up." *Not depending on you is how he tries to collaborate with you!*

In an insecure attachment, he learned to collaborate with caretakers by not depending. This behavior occurs automatically and habitually. He does not do it on purpose. Nor does he do it consciously. However, as an adult, this form of relating makes him lonely, anxious, and depressed.

What his caretakers considered collaboration, you might mistakenly call resistance. But he may never have had a relationship where another form of relationship was possible. That's why co-creating a healing relationship takes persistence and patience.

What do we mean by patience? Accept him as he is with his conflicts, problems, and relational patterns. Then you can form a healing relationship. If you reject the patient you have, he will have to drop out to find a therapist who can accept him and his problematic behaviors. To work effectively, we must accept reality: the patient as he is with the conflicts he has.

Relating, Not Just Intervening

These skill-building exercises will teach you many techniques. A technique usually refers to a procedure applied to an object to achieve a specific result. But in therapy, techniques refer to the ways we connect with patients who fear connecting. We do not *do* a technique to a patient. Rather, psychotherapy interventions are *how we relate, how we work together*. Do not try out a technique; offer a relationship. We intervene to build a healing therapeutic alliance. Let's develop those relational skills!

CHAPTER TWO

How to Use These Exercises
to Become More Skillful

To develop skills, we must engage in deliberate practice. What happens if we don't? Standard psychotherapy training causes no change in trainees' outcomes with patients (Nyman, Nafzinger, and Smith 2011). Ninety-three percent of psychotherapy supervision is inadequate, and 35 percent is harmful (Ellis et al. 2014)! As a result, 70 percent of therapists after graduation say that they lack the skills to motivate patients to work hard in therapy and don't know how to use specific techniques for specific patients (Orlinsky and Ronnestad 2005). And in that study, how many of these highly educated and experienced clinicians felt a sense of mastery? Fewer than 47 percent.

Other fields also find that students acquire theoretical knowledge but not practical skills. Many studies show that medical school training results in substandard clinical skill acquisition among physicians (Joorabchi and Devries 1996; Lypson et al. 2004; McGaghie and Kristopaitis 2015; Cohen et al. 2013; Wilcox et al. 2014; Bell et al. 2009). Clinical experience during training does not guarantee clinical competence (Kyser et al. 2014; Ericsson 2014).

Age, gender, experience, and degree do not correlate with patient outcome in psychotherapy (Chow et al. 2015). Only one therapist factor correlates with patient outcome: the time spent practicing specific clinical skills (Chow et al. 2015). However, psychotherapy training often focuses primarily on learning theory, not gaining clinical skills. To address this problem, medical schools have developed simulation-based learning models for residents. Practicing specific skills led to dramatic improvements in skill mastery that traditional teaching settings did not achieve (McGaghie et al. 2014).

This book uses a simulation-based learning model to develop your mastery of specific clinical skills. We use the expert performance model (McGaghie and Kristopaitis 2015) to define the key skills of experts. Having studied videotapes of expert psychotherapists, we discerned their specific relational skills. Then we developed exercises to build those skills.

For each exercise, you will learn a piece of theory, and then you will learn a specific skill based on that theory. After that, you will practice each skill until you have mastered it. Each new skill builds on previous skills. And you will learn the skills in the order in which you usually use them when developing a therapeutic alliance. This way, over time, you will master clinical skills of increasing complexity and difficulty.

Practicing specific, structured skill-building exercises gives you objective feedback on your progress. As you progress through the book, you will learn over forty skills that experts use when establishing a working alliance. By working through the exercises, you will learn which of your skills are strong and which you can improve, and by practicing, you will master those relational skills one at a time. The more you practice, the greater your mastery and the deeper your understanding will be.

Mastery-based learning has improved clinical skills in cardiac life support (Wayne et al. 2006), paracentesis (Barsuk et al. 2012), and central venous catheter insertion (Barsuk et al. 2009). However, it has never been used for the development of psychiatric skills. A pilot study (Frederickson et al. 2019) with drug counselors at an inpatient drug rehabilitation program found that targeted skill-building exercises for therapists reduced dropout rates from 40 percent to 23 percent in ten weeks. Six-month sobriety after treatment for the control group was 17 percent but 48.8 percent for the experimental group. These studies suggest that skill-building for therapists can improve patient outcomes.

Further, by practicing these skills, you will experience yourself, your patient, and the therapeutic role in new ways. When linked with your previous explicit knowledge, this implicit knowledge will make you a more skilled and flexible therapist, which will lead to improved outcomes (Vacoch and Strupp 2000). It is not enough to know theory; you must know how to put it into practice.

Why practice? To become more skillful and effective. Whether we are a musician, ballet dancer, or psychotherapist, we have the chance to practice basic skills until they are automatic. Yet, once mastered, we can apply our skills flexibly for good outcomes (Truijens et al. 2019). And as any musician can tell you, this persistent hard work is not easy. But the evidence is clear: people who practice specific skills constantly become more skilled (Ericsson 2014). Psychotherapy is no exception.

Deliberately practicing specific relational skills differs from the usual way we study. Usually, we can read a book, remember it, and write answers on a test. That's cognitive mastery. But to put theory into practice, we must be able to assess the patient's problem and intervene right away, not next week. The patient needs help now. And it takes practice to develop these quick assessment and intervention skills. You can't learn to play the guitar by only reading a book. You must pick up the guitar and practice playing it—a lot. Likewise, you can't learn to heal patients only by reading. You must practice skills to become skillful.

HOW TO IMPROVE AS A THERAPIST: GUIDELINES FOR USING THESE SKILL-BUILDING EXERCISES

"How do you get to Carnegie Hall?" "Practice, practice, practice!" To become skilled like musicians, chess masters, and ballerinas, we can practice skills just like they do. We start with basic skills and practice them repeatedly until we master them. If our basic skills are weak, we will have a weak foundation. Even skilled musicians, martial artists, and professional athletes practice basic skills as part of their daily warm-up.

Thus, this book starts with fundamental skills and leads gradually to more complex ones, each building on the other. Through stages, each chapter takes you through skills in the order in which you will need them in therapy:

1. Regulating anxiety so therapy is a safe place to explore
2. Helping the patient declare a problem to work on
3. Helping the patient declare his will to work on the problem
4. Deactivating misperceptions of the therapist or therapy
5. Building motivation to work toward a positive goal
6. Getting consensus on the therapeutic task

Don't jump around. Start with the beginning exercises and work your way through the book. Then your skills and understanding will develop in a stepwise, integrated fashion.

Since these skills involve cognitive and relational learning, we offer two forms of practice—both of which are necessary for optimal learning: (1) audio practice by yourself in a recording with me (Jon Frederickson) and (2) role-play practice with another person. The audio practice method will help you master the skills cognitively. The role-playing studies will help you learn relationally when you play both the therapist and the patient roles. Playing the therapist role with a colleague or fellow student will strengthen your ability to maintain a consistent therapeutic focus with your patients. Playing the patient role will strengthen your ability to identify with her experience of therapy.

Audio Practicing While Alone

For audio practicing, you will read the initial material about the skill in this book. Then click on the audio link for the skill. As the recording plays, you will listen to me, Jon Frederickson. First, I will describe the relational skill we will work on together, and I will teach you the principle behind it. Then I will offer a sample answer so you will know how to intervene. Next, you and I will begin the skill-building exercise: I will play the patient, and you will play the therapist. On the first exercise, you will ask, "What is the problem you would like me to help you with?" Then I will offer a patient response, and you will intervene. After your intervention, I will provide the suggested therapist response. Then we will go to the following example, repeating the same pattern with you asking for the problem. That's it.

As you repeat each exercise, you will understand the relational pattern the patient offers, and you will get better at inviting a secure relationship. After you have gone through an exercise once, do it again. No basketball player ever learned how to shoot baskets after a single shot or even ten shots. Repetition helps you improve until you reach 100 percent accuracy. Then you won't have to think so hard about what you are going to say before you say it. And you can be more present with your patient. When interventions occur to you easily, you can relate to the patient more flexibly and thoughtfully.

Repeating these skills also helps you experience the patient's relational struggle. They allow you to feel yourself relating to the patient, consciously inviting a therapeutic alliance. With every skill, you invite him to have a therapeutic alliance with you where depending, having problems, and needing help are normal, usual, and human.

Practice each skill repeatedly until you master it (Ericsson 2008). Then you can assess quickly how to intervene in therapy without losing focus while searching in your head for responses you can't remember. And you will be more effective the next time that problem comes up in therapy. Your work will automatically improve. Each skill you master builds the foundation for more complex skills. If your initial relational skills are shaky, the later phases of alliance-building will be too. So, master these skills one at a time to build a firm foundation for your growing expertise.

You can practice these audio skill-building exercises anytime you want, for example, while riding your bike or driving your car. We all have downtime we aren't using. That's an ideal time to practice your skill-building without adding any burden to your day. Many students have made their commutes more enjoyable by practicing their skills while on the freeway.

Role-Play Practice with Another Person

You can also practice these skills through role-playing with a fellow student or colleague. The person who plays the patient role will read the patient scripts in this book. The person who plays the therapist role will not look at the script but will try to intervene using the skills learned from the book. If the therapist has trouble, the patient will read the suggested answer from the book, and then the two of you can repeat that exercise. Since you, as the therapist, do not have the script, you have to figure out how to respond—like you would have to with a patient. When you are in the therapist role, do not read the script during the exercise. Why? You will get better at reading, not intervening. These skill-building exercises help you relate without a script, just like you have to during therapy. If you find a particular skill difficult, read it together once with your colleague who plays the patient. Then have your colleague read the patient script while you respond as the therapist without the script. Practice that exercise several times until you have mastered it.

First, the person in the patient role reads the script to you, the therapist, and gives you the instructions. Then the person in the patient role tells you, the therapist, how to start. For example, if you are playing the therapist, you might ask, "What is the problem you would like me to help you with?" The person in the patient role then responds, and you intervene. If you make a mistake, your partner can read the suggested answer to give you immediate feedback. And then you can go on to ask the next question.

See how to do these skill-building exercises with a partner at HTRBook.com/IntroBV.

After the first time through, the two of you should do the same exercise a few more times *without any additional talking or commentary*. Try to recreate the situation you will face in therapy by maintaining a consistent therapeutic focus without stopping until you and the patient have achieved the next step in building the alliance. If the two of you start to chat, you won't get the in vivo exposure you need: working on a problem consistently until the patient can move to the next step. Chatting during skill-building helps you learn to chat, not to build your skills. So, keep focused on the task: doing skill-building exercises without stopping.

The person who plays the patient role should act like that patient, using facial gestures and vocal tones. Then you, as the therapist, will receive more in vivo exposure as you learn how to keep intervening effectively without stopping. Continue until you reach the end of the exercise. If you have trouble, the person in the patient role can offer the suggested answer (that's in italics) to help you understand the principle of the exercise. Then, after the first time through, do the exercise again without stopping. For mastery, you must be able to address patient responses as quickly as they occur in therapy.

Repetition is the key to achieving mastery in all arts and crafts. Once you can do these exercises automatically without thinking, your mind will be free to think about other aspects of the patient and the relationship. And repetition will also teach you to persist patiently when the patient has trouble.

No matter what kind of therapy we do, we must accomplish certain tasks to form a working relationship. The patient must declare a problem to work on, and her anxiety needs to be regulated to do the work. The patient must want to do therapy and relate to you realistically. Otherwise, she will have a misalliance with a misperception. When the patient has a positive goal that makes therapy worthwhile, it will motivate her to do therapy. The following skills are based on transtheoretical principles of therapy. You can incorporate these skills into any treatment model. Practice, practice, practice! Don't stop until you have mastered each exercise 100 percent. Now we'll go to the skills.

CHAPTER THREE

Co-Creating Safety to Make It Safe to Depend

When we invite a patient to tell us her problem so we can help her, we invite her to depend upon us. But what if in her past depending brought pain instead of relief? What if it was not safe for her to depend on her loved ones? Then the dangers of the past cast a shadow on the therapy. The patient may know you are safe, but her bodily anxiety may make her feel unsafe. If so, we need to identify and regulate her anxiety first so she can feel safe with you. Only then will she be able to depend on you and do the work of therapy.

Principle for High Anxiety:
Identify and regulate anxiety to co-create a sense of safety in a secure attachment.

WHEN DECLARING A PROBLEM TRIGGERS TOO MUCH ANXIETY

To develop a therapeutic alliance, we ask about the problem for which the patient seeks our help. Sometimes patients can tell us right away. However, some patients immediately become anxious, even before they have declared a problem. Why? When you invite a person to declare a problem, you invite him to depend upon you. Yet, for many patients, depending in the past led to harm rather than help. As a result, declaring a problem may trigger too much anxiety for the therapy to feel safe. Thus, sometimes we must regulate anxiety first to make the patient feel safe enough to reveal a problem. The first exercises show how to form a therapeutic alliance with patients whose anxiety becomes too high. By regulating anxiety together, we can co-create a sense of safety. Then the work of therapy becomes possible.

See a demonstration of how to help patients regulate their anxiety at HTRBook.com/Video-1.

STAGE ONE: REGULATING ANXIETY

The following exercise will help you assess the patient's anxiety.

Skill-Building Exercise One: Assessing How Anxiety Appears in the Body

Principle: *When you ask for a problem to work on, assess anxiety to ensure it is not too high.*

Anxiety is not a thought in your mind; it's an experience in your body. We *feel* anxious. When our brain perceives a risk, the somatic and autonomic nervous systems activate our bodies to respond. They create the bodily symptoms of anxiety (Robertson et al. 2004).

When anxiety is regulated, it is triggered by the somatic nervous system, creating symptoms such as clenched hands, tension headaches, tension in the back and neck, and sighing (Abbass 2015; Davanloo 2002–2004; Frederickson 2013, 2021; Porges 2011; Robertson et al. 2004). The somatic nervous system makes our voluntary muscles tense up. Anytime we do something new or unfamiliar, we become anxious. Naturally, patients will be anxious in therapy when they face what they usually avoid. As a result, our goal is not the absence of anxiety but rather anxiety that is regulated while the patient explores difficult issues. That means anxiety in the somatic nervous system.

However, when anxiety is too high, the parasympathetic nervous system triggers anxiety symptoms such as migraine headaches, stomachaches, nausea, diarrhea, and the need to go to the bathroom. And when it is even more severe, patients suffer from symptoms such as dizziness, loss of memory, problems thinking, blurry vision, and ringing in the ears (Abbass 2015; Frederickson 2013; Porges 2011; Robertson et al. 2004). The parasympathetic nervous system activates smooth muscles in our digestive tract and blood vessels, creating many of these severe anxiety symptoms.

When anxiety is in the somatic nervous system, it is low. Therefore, you can explore the patient's problems freely. However, it is too high when anxiety is in the parasympathetic nervous system. The patient will not feel safe enough to form a therapeutic alliance. Thus, we need to regulate the patient's anxiety.

Many anxious patients cannot regulate their anxiety. After all, their caretakers often *caused* the patient's anxiety; they didn't regulate it. If patients grew up with people who ignored their anxiety, they often ignore it too. They are not used to someone trying to regulate their anxiety; they are used to people making them anxious. That's why your offer to pay attention to and regulate anxiety will seem strange to many patients.

To learn how to regulate the patient's anxiety, we need to assess whether her anxiety is too high. Anxiety in the somatic nervous system does not need to be regulated. Those symptoms include the following:

- Tension
- Clenching hands
- Sighing

Anxiety in the parasympathetic nervous system needs to be regulated. Those symptoms include the following:

- Migraine headaches
- Stomachaches
- Nausea
- Diarrhea
- The need to go to the bathroom
- Cognitive/perceptual disruption
- Dizziness
- Loss of memory
- Problems thinking
- Blurry vision
- Ringing in the ears

Watch an exercise on how to determine the patient's level of anxiety at HTRBook.com/Video-2. Practice assessing where anxiety is discharged in the body at HTRBook.com/Audio-1.

As the patient in this role-play exercise, read the following to your partner who is in the therapist role. "You will ask me what the problem is I would like help with. I will play the patient and offer an anxiety response. You, as the therapist, will assess whether the anxiety is going into the somatic nervous system, not needing regulation, or parasympathetic nervous system, needing regulation. Then you will ask your question again, I'll offer another anxiety symptom, and you'll assess it. And we'll keep doing that for a series of responses. Go ahead and ask, 'What is the problem you would like me to help you with?'"

Patient Response	Partner's Assessment of the Response
Sigh.	Somatic nervous system, regulated
"I am getting sick to my stomach."	Parasympathetic nervous system, needs regulation
"I need to go to the bathroom."	Parasympathetic nervous system, needs regulation
Sigh.	Somatic nervous system, regulated
"I feel tense in my neck."	Somatic nervous system, regulated
"I'm getting a slight migraine headache."	Parasympathetic nervous system, needs regulation
"I'm feeling dizzy."	Parasympathetic nervous system, needs regulation
"I'm feeling a little nauseous."	Parasympathetic nervous system, needs regulation
Sigh.	Somatic nervous system, regulated
"My vision is getting blurry."	Parasympathetic nervous system, needs regulation
"I feel tension in my stomach."	Somatic nervous system, regulated
"What did you say?"	Parasympathetic nervous system, needs regulation
"Is there something wrong with this chair? My back is so tense!"	Somatic nervous system, regulated
"I need to go to the bathroom."	Parasympathetic nervous system, needs regulation
"My ears are ringing."	Parasympathetic nervous system, needs regulation
"I'm getting a tension headache."	Somatic nervous system, regulated

Now let's continue the role-play exercise. The person in the patient role should read the following to the person in the therapist role. When you ask for the problem and the patient is already too anxious, regulate the patient's anxiety before asking about the problem again. The patient's body has already told you his first problem: his anxiety is too high and needs to be regulated. These symptoms will tell you whether you need to regulate anxiety. Let's do this exercise again. When you have done it three times, we'll change roles so I can master this exercise too. Repetition can seem boring. But if we practice this several times, we will be calmer and more effective when assessing our patients' anxiety in the session."

Questions to ask each other to strengthen your skills: Now that you know specific physical signs of when anxiety is too high, how does this change your understanding of anxiety and how to regulate it? Now that you understand that anxiety is not a thought in the head but a physical experience in the body, how does this change your previous understanding of anxiety? And now that you understand that asking for help can trigger high anxiety, how does this change your understanding of what it means for the patient to depend on you?

Skill-Building Exercise Two: Identifying and Regulating Anxiety

When patients are too anxious, we need to develop an anxiety-regulating relationship so that therapy becomes a safe place. To form a secure attachment, the patient must feel safe *with you*. For anxious patients, we do that by regulating anxiety.

We start by finding out where the patient feels anxious in the body. Then we know whether it is safe to explore the problem or whether we need to regulate anxiety first.

Watch a demonstration of how to assess anxiety at HTRBook.com/Video-3.

We can regulate their anxiety by identifying an anxiety symptom as a sign of anxiety. Then we can describe the process: "When I asked about your problem, you became anxious, and the anxiety made you dizzy. Do you see that sequence too?" Therapy feels safer when we can show the patient why her anxiety makes sense. Now the patient learns that the therapist is not a threat, as people were in her past. What makes her anxious now is her wish to depend on another person. Describing the sequence that caused her anxiety symptoms brings her anxiety down until she sighs, tenses up, or intellectualizes again. Once anxiety is in this tolerable range, we can explore the problem.

Although these signs of anxiety may be new to you, if you ask patients about these symptoms, you will learn that a surprising number of patients try to do therapy when they are too anxious to do it. Many patients in outpatient clinics, hospitals, or drug rehabilitation facilities suffer from excessive anxiety. If you identify and regulate their anxiety, they can finally benefit from therapy. And you will have shown them that therapy can be a safe place.

Help the patient see the sequence of causality: (1) declaring a problem, (2) triggers anxiety, and (3) results in an anxiety symptom.

When she sees this sequence, her symptoms make sense, and she will calm down. If she does not see that declaring a problem makes her anxious, she could mistakenly think you cause her anxiety, and then she might drop out of therapy. However, if you can help her see that declaring a problem and asking for help makes her anxious, she will understand. Then you will have begun to form a relationship for change.

Watch a demonstration of how to help patients recognize the cause of their anxiety at HTRBook .com/Video-4.

Practice a skill-building exercise on helping the patient understand what causes his anxiety at HTRBook.com/Audio-2.

As the patient in this role-play exercise, read the following to your partner who is in the therapist role: "In this skill-building exercise, you will help me as the patient understand what causes my anxiety. Each time you will ask, 'What is the problem you would like me to help you with?'" Here's how the role-play will unfold.

Pt: I am feeling anxious.

Th: Where do you notice feeling this anxiety in your body?

Pt: I feel shaky.

Th: This shakiness is a sign of anxiety. I asked about your problem. Something about my asking about your problem triggered this anxiety, and the anxiety makes your body shaky. Do you notice that sequence too?

Principle: *Identify anxiety and describe causality (asking about a problem triggers anxiety symptoms) to regulate anxiety.*

As the patient in this role-play exercise, read the following to your partner who is in the therapist role: "You will ask me, 'What is the problem you would like me to help you with?' I will respond with anxiety. Ask me where I feel the anxiety in my body. When I answer, identify my symptom as anxiety and then regulate my anxiety by showing me that declaring a problem triggered my anxiety. Go ahead and ask me, 'What is the problem you would like me to help you with?'"

Role-Play One

Pt: I feel anxious.

Th: Where do you notice feeling anxiety in your body?

Pt: I am getting sick to my stomach. [*"This is a sign of anxiety. I asked about the problem you would like me to help you with. Describing a problem makes you anxious. And the anxiety makes you sick to your stomach. Do you see what I mean?"*]

Role-Play Two

Th: What is the problem you would like me to help you with?

Pt: I feel anxious.

Th: Where do you notice feeling anxiety in your body?

Pt: [*Sighs.*] I feel tense in my stomach. [*"That's a sign of anxiety. So, what is the problem you would like me to help you with?" When anxiety is in the somatic nervous system, we can keep exploring. You do not need to regulate anxiety when it is in the somatic nervous system.*]

Role-Play Three

Th: What is the problem you would like me to help you with?

Pt: I feel anxious.

Th: Where do you notice feeling anxiety in your body?

Pt: I need to go to the bathroom. [*"This is a sign of anxiety. I asked about the problem you would like me to help you with. Describing a problem makes you anxious. And the anxiety makes you need to go to the bathroom. Do you see what I mean?"*]

Role-Play Four

Th: What is the problem you would like me to help you with?

Pt: I feel anxious.

Th: Where do you notice feeling anxiety in your body?

Pt: I'm getting a slight migraine headache. [*"This is a sign of anxiety. I asked about the problem you would like me to help you with. Describing a problem makes you anxious. And the anxiety gives you a migraine headache. Do you see what I mean?"*]

Role-Play Five

Th: What is the problem you would like me to help you with?

Pt: I feel anxious.

Th: Where do you notice feeling anxiety in your body?

Pt: [*Sighs*] I'm getting a tension headache. [*"That's often a sign of anxiety. So, what is the problem you would like me to help you with?" When anxiety is in the somatic nervous system, it does not need to be regulated. We can keep exploring.*]

Role-Play Six

Th: What is the problem you would like me to help you with?

Pt: I feel anxious.

Th: Where do you notice feeling anxiety in your body?

Pt: I'm feeling dizzy. [*"This is a sign of anxiety. I asked about the problem you would like me to help you with. Describing a problem makes you anxious. And the anxiety makes you dizzy. Do you see what I mean?"*]

Role-Play Seven

Th: What is the problem you would like me to help you with?

Pt: I'm feeling a little nauseous. [*"This is a sign of anxiety. I asked about the problem you would like me to help you with. Describing a problem makes you anxious. And the anxiety makes you nauseous. Do you see what I mean?"*]

Role-Play Eight

Th: What is the problem you would like me to help you with?

Pt: I feel anxious.

Th: Where do you notice feeling anxiety in your body?

Pt: My vision is getting blurry. [*"This is a sign of anxiety. I asked about the problem you would like me to help you with. Describing a problem makes you anxious. And the anxiety makes your vision blurry. Do you see what I mean?"*]

Role-Play Nine

Th: What is the problem you would like me to help you with?

Pt: I have an upset stomach. [*"This can be a sign of anxiety. I asked about the problem you would like me to help you with. Describing a problem makes you anxious. And the anxiety makes you have an upset stomach. Do you see what I mean?"*]

Role-Play Ten

Th: What is the problem you would like me to help you with?

Pt: I feel anxious.

Th: Where do you notice feeling anxiety in your body?

Pt: My ears are ringing. [*"This is a sign of anxiety. I asked about the problem you would like me to help you with. Describing a problem makes you anxious, and the anxiety makes your ears ring. Do you see what I mean?"*]

The sooner the patient can recognize an anxiety symptom, the sooner she can regulate it. Now therapy becomes a safe place with an anxiety-regulating therapist. Then together, the therapist and patient can look at the problem that triggered the patient's anxiety. Regulating anxiety helps co-create a sense of safety.

Now let's continue the role-play exercise. The person in the patient role should read the following to the person in the therapist role. "Let's do the exercise again. Whenever you intervene,

I, as the patient, will go immediately to the next patient statement. Let's make this exercise feel like a real session. We won't stop for chitchat. We'll go straight through so you get the experience of processing and intervening more quickly. We'll repeat it several times. After you master this exercise, we'll shift roles so I can master it too."

Questions to ask each other to strengthen your skills: How are these exercises changing how you assess whether anxiety is too high? What do you understand now that you did not understand before you did these anxiety exercises? What do you understand now about the relationship between having anxiety and depending on a therapist for help? Are you the danger, or has depending been dangerous for her? How does that change your understanding of the patient's plight? How do you experience your partner as an anxiety regulator? What suggestions could you offer your partner about the quality of the caring relationship being offered? How could your partner be more anxiety-regulating as a therapist?

See how validating anxiety affects the patient at HTRBook.com/Video-5.

Skill-Building Exercise Three: Regulating Anxiety by Paying Attention to an Anxiety Symptom

---

Principle: *Invite the patient to pay attention to an anxiety symptom to regulate anxiety.*

Now we will look at another way to regulate anxiety: directing the patient's attention to an anxiety symptom. Patients who grew up in an insecure attachment regulated their caretakers by hiding and ignoring their anxiety. Thus, to form a secure attachment, we teach patients to pay attention to the anxiety they usually ignore. Traumatic relationships cause anxiety; healing relationships regulate it.

Practice a skill-building exercise on regulating anxiety at HTRBook.com/Audio-3.

For this role-play exercise, read the following to your partner who is in the therapist role. "In this example, you will ask me about the problem I would like you to help me with. Again, I will respond with anxiety. First, identify my anxiety and then invite me to pay attention to an anxiety symptom. For example, when I respond with anxiety in the form of nausea, you could say: 'This is a sign of anxiety. Shall we see if we can regulate your anxiety? As you pay attention to that symptom in your stomach, what do you notice feeling in your stomach?'

"Now start the role-play exercise. Ask me, 'What is the problem you would like me to help you with?' Go ahead."

Pt: I am getting sick to my stomach. [*"This is a sign of anxiety. Shall we see if we can regulate your anxiety? As you pay attention to that symptom in your stomach, what do you notice feeling in your stomach?" Paying attention to an anxiety symptom often reduces and regulates the anxiety.*]

Pt: [*Sighs.*] I feel tense in my stomach. [*"Something about declaring a problem gets you anxious and tense. If we look under the tension, what is the problem you would like me to help you with?" When anxiety is in the somatic nervous system, it does not need to be regulated. You can explore safely.*]

Pt: I need to go to the bathroom. [*"This can be a sign of anxiety. Shall we see if we can regulate your anxiety? As you pay attention to that symptom in your stomach, what do you notice feeling in your stomach?"*]

Pt: I'm getting a slight migraine headache. [*"This can be a sign of anxiety. Shall we see if we can regulate your anxiety? As you pay attention to that symptom in your head, what do you notice feeling there?"*]

Pt: [*Sighs.*] I'm getting a tension headache. [*"Something about sharing a problem gets you tensed up. If we look underneath the tension, what is the problem you would like me to help you with?" When anxiety is in the somatic nervous system, keep exploring. There is no need to regulate anxiety.*]

Pt: I'm feeling dizzy. [*"This is a sign of anxiety. Shall we see if we can regulate your anxiety? As you pay attention to that symptom in your head, what do you notice feeling there?"*]

Pt: I'm feeling a little nauseous. [*"This is a sign of anxiety. Shall we see if we can regulate your anxiety? As you pay attention to that symptom in your stomach, what do you notice feeling in your stomach?"*]

Pt: My vision is getting blurry. [*"This is a sign of anxiety. Shall we see if we can regulate your anxiety? As you pay attention to that symptom of blurry vision, what else do you notice feeling in your body?"*]

Pt: My ears are ringing. [*"This is a sign of anxiety. Shall we see if we can regulate your anxiety? As you pay attention to that symptom of ringing ears, what else do you notice feeling physically in your body?"*]

Now let's continue the role-play exercise. The person in the patient role should read the following to the person in the therapist role. "Let's do the exercise again. Whenever you intervene, I, as the patient, will go immediately to the next patient statement. Let's make this exercise feel like a real session. We won't stop for chitchat. We'll go straight through so you get the experience of processing and intervening more quickly. We'll repeat it several times. After you master this exercise, we'll shift roles so I can master it too."

Questions to ask each other to strengthen your skills: What did you learn by being in the patient role? How does practicing this anxiety regulation skill for several minutes change your understanding of being an anxiety-regulating therapist? How is focusing on the patient's body changing how you used to focus on the patient's anxiety? What are you learning from each other about the role of your tone of voice in anxiety regulation? What suggestions could you offer your partner to be more anxiety regulating? How do you experience the quality of the relationship your partner offers the patient? What suggestions could you offer your partner about the quality of the caring relationship being offered? How could your partner be more anxiety-regulating as a therapist?

Skill-Building Exercise Four: Helping Patients Pay Attention to Rather Than Ignore Anxiety So They Can Regulate It

Principle: *Point out an anxiety symptom, then block the strategy of ignoring it by inviting the patient to pay attention to anxiety.*

Regulating anxiety works for most patients. But when it doesn't, an avoidance strategy usually perpetuates the anxiety. When this happens, we can help the patient see and let go of strategies that perpetuate her anxiety. Then we can help her regulate it.

One strategy that prevents anxiety regulation is ignoring anxiety. In traumatic insecure attachments, caretakers ignore, dismiss, and neglect the child's anxiety. So, the child does too. But then, as an adult, the patient can't regulate her anxiety. As a result, her anxiety remains too high, and she can't think properly. She can't remember what you say. She can't concentrate. For instance, you ask, "What's the problem you would like me to help you with?"

Pt: I've got some issues. [*Patient's leg is shaking.*]

Th: I notice your leg is shaking. That can be a sign of anxiety. Are you aware of feeling anxious right now?

Pt: I'm always anxious. It's no big deal.

Th: Could we take a look at your anxiety so we could help you bring it down? [*Block the dismissal of her anxiety ("It's no big deal.") by inviting the patient to form a healing relationship where we regulate anxiety together.*]

When patients ignore their anxiety, block this strategy and invite them to pay attention to their anxiety to regulate it. We can co-create a safe place in therapy only if we pay attention to anxiety together and regulate it. This is how we co-create a healing relationship.

Practice a role-play exercise on helping patients identify their anxiety at HTRBook.com/Audio-4.

As the patient in this role-play exercise, read the following to your partner who is in the therapist role. "In the following role-play, you will ask, 'What is the problem you would like me to help you with?' Each time, as your patient, I will respond with anxiety. You will ask: 'Are you aware of feeling anxious right now?' In each case, I will ignore, neglect, dismiss, talk over, or minimize my anxiety. Help me see my anxiety, and then block my ignoring strategy by inviting me to pay attention to my anxiety.

Learn how to help patients recognize and pay attention to their anxiety at HTRBook.com /Video-6.

Go ahead and start the role-play exercise. Ask, "What's the problem you would like me to help you with?"

Role-Play One

Pt: I'm a little dizzy.

Th: That's a sign of anxiety. Are you aware of feeling anxious right now?

Pt: Oh, I'm used to that. [*"I'm sure you are. Shall we take a look at your anxiety and see if we can regulate it so you don't have to get dizzy?"*]

Role-Play Two

Th: What's the problem you would like me to help you with?

Pt: I am getting sick to my stomach.

Th: That can be a sign of anxiety. Are you aware of feeling anxious right now?

Pt: It's not so bad. [*"Sickness in your stomach is a sign of severe anxiety. Could we take a look at your anxiety and see if we can regulate it so you don't have to feel sick to your stomach?"*]

Role-Play Three

Th: What's the problem you would like me to help you with?

Pt: [*Patient stares glassy-eyed at the therapist.*] How do I know if you can help me?

Th: Let's see if we can find out. Are you aware of feeling anxious right now?

Pt: I feel really uncomfortable. But I guess I'll have to get used to that. [*"Feeling uncomfortable is a sign of anxiety. Shall we take a look at your anxiety so we could help you bring it down? Then you won't have to get used to it."*]

Role-Play Four

Th: What's the problem you would like me to help you with?

Pt: [*Patient rubs her head.*] I'm getting a slight migraine headache.

Th: That can be a sign of anxiety. Are you aware of feeling anxious right now?

Pt: Oh, it's nothing. My doctor gives me medication for it. I just forgot to take the pills before I came here. [*"This headache can be a sign of anxiety. Shall we take a look at your anxiety and see if we can regulate it? That can sometimes make a migraine come down."*]

Role-Play Five

Th: What's the problem you would like me to help you with?

Pt: [*Patient looks scared.*]

Th: Are you aware of feeling anxious right now?

Pt: Yes. But that's not what I want to talk about. [*"Of course not. But if we don't talk about your anxiety, you will feel uncomfortable here, and I don't want you to feel uncomfortable. Could we take a look at your anxiety so we could help you bring it down?"*]

Role-Play Six

Th: What's the problem you would like me to help you with?

Pt: I'm not sure I feel comfortable talking about it.

Th: That can be a sign of anxiety. Are you feeling anxious right now?

Pt: I'm feeling nauseous. But I really don't want to pay attention to that. If I pay attention to it, it will just get worse. [*"This nausea is a sign of anxiety. When you say that you don't want to pay attention to it, my concern is that your anxiety will get worse. Could we pay attention to it and see if we could bring it down? Then the therapy will feel a lot more comfortable."*]

Role-Play Seven

Th: What's the problem you would like me to help you with?

Pt: I'm not sure I feel comfortable talking about it.

Th: That can be a sign of anxiety. Are you aware of feeling anxious in your body right now?

Pt: I feel sick to my stomach.

Th: That's a sign of anxiety.

Pt: I'm anxious all the time. My doctor says I need to relax, but I can't. [*"A sick stomach is a sign of anxiety. Since you can't relax, could we take a look at your anxiety so we can help you bring it down?"*]

Role-Play Eight

Th: What's the problem you would like me to help you with?

Pt: What did you say? My mind just blanked out.

Th: That can be a sign of anxiety. Are you aware of feeling anxious right now?

Pt: Oh, my mind does that all the time. [*"Blanking out is a sign of high anxiety. Could we take a look at your anxiety so we could help you bring it down so your mind wouldn't blank out?"*]

Role-Play Nine

Th: What's the problem you would like me to help you with?

Pt: I'm so tired. If I tried to stand up right now, I'm not sure my legs would hold me up.

Th: That can be a sign of anxiety. Are you aware of feeling anxious right now?

Pt: Well, as long as I'm sitting here, it's no big deal. [*"This is a sign of high anxiety. If we treat it like it's no big deal, your anxiety could get worse. Could we take a look at your anxiety instead so we could help you bring it down?"*]

Role-Play Ten

Th: What's the problem you would like me to help you with?

Pt: I'm just really anxious.

Th: How do you experience this anxiety physically in your body?

Pt: My ears are ringing, but I can still hear you. Sometimes I can't even hear other people. [*"This problem with hearing is a sign of high anxiety. Could we take a look at your anxiety and see if we can regulate it so your ears don't ring?"*]

You can't regulate the patient's anxiety by yourself. You and the patient can only do it together. That's how we co-create a sense of safety in therapy. In an insecure attachment, the patient hides her anxiety to regulate the other person's anxiety. In a secure attachment, the therapist encourages the patient to reveal her anxiety so that together we can pay attention to it and regulate it. By doing so, the therapist lets the patient know, "You don't have to hide your anxiety to protect me. Let's pay attention to your anxiety so we can help you feel safe again." The patient often cannot regulate her anxiety by herself. She needs our help. Together we can do what she cannot do alone.

As long as you help the patient return to her anxiety so she can regulate it, your answer will be fine. The goal here is not to repeat the words in the book but to learn the principle guiding those words: block the ignoring of anxiety so the patient can pay attention to the anxiety.

Now let's continue the role-play exercise. The person in the patient role should read the following to the person in the therapist role. "Let's do the exercise again. Whenever you intervene, I, as the patient, will go immediately to the next patient statement. Let's make this exercise feel like a real session. We won't stop for chitchat. We'll go straight through so you get the experience of processing and intervening more quickly. We'll repeat it several times. After you master this exercise, we'll shift roles so I can master it too."

Questions to ask each other to strengthen your skills: What are you learning about how ignoring anxiety prevents its regulation? How does this exercise change your understanding of what prevents patients from regulating their anxiety? How did you experience the therapist's encouragements to pay attention to your anxiety? How did this exercise change your understanding of the complexities of anxiety regulation? Does your partner sound caring or distant? What suggestions might you offer your partner so that this feels like a caring relationship? How could your partner be more anxiety-regulating as a therapist?

Skill-Building Exercise Five: Blocking Strategies That Prevent Anxiety Regulation and Then Regulating Anxiety

Principle: *Block the strategy against paying attention to anxiety and invite the patient to pay attention to her anxiety.*

When patients ignore their anxiety, it remains chronically elevated, and they cannot regulate it. Thus, we need to interrupt any avoidance strategy that prevents the patient from paying attention to and regulating his anxiety. The patient is not aware of these automatic and habitual strategies. So, be patient and compassionate. These are just habits he learned to protect others from his anxiety.

Learn to be an anxiety-regulating presence by watching HTRBook.com/Video-7.

Practice a role-play exercise on blocking avoidance strategies at HTRBook.com/Audio-5.

As the patient in this role-play exercise, read the following to your partner who is in the therapist role. "In the following role-play exercises, you, as the therapist, will ask me, 'Are you aware of feeling anxious?' In the patient role, I will avoid paying attention to my anxiety. First, block my avoidance strategy and then invite me to pay attention to my anxiety.

"Go ahead and start the role-play exercise by asking, 'Are you aware of feeling anxious?'"

Role-Play One

Th: Are you aware of feeling anxious?

Pt: [*Speaking rapidly*] Oh yes, doctor, I feel tremendous anxiety in my whole body, from my feet to my head. I think I even feel it in the pores of my skin. Oh, doctor, it's absolutely horrible. I can't stand it; it's growing and growing constantly. . . . [*"Do you notice how you talk rapidly now? That's often a sign of anxiety. Could we pay attention to your anxiety now and see if we can help you with it?" In this example, when the patient speaks rapidly, make sure you speak very slowly to slow down and calm her. Be the calm you want her to feel. Repeat this example several times until the therapist can speak slowly and calmly when the patient speaks quickly and anxiously.*]

Role-Play Two

Th: Are you aware of feeling anxious?

Pt: Before we get to that, can you give me medication? I'm really having trouble with withdrawal. [*"I can arrange for you to get medication if you need it after the session. To help you right now, can we take a look at your anxiety and see if we can help you with it?"*]

Role-Play Three

Th: Are you aware of feeling anxious?

Pt: Can you help me, doctor? [*"I'd be glad to. To help you now, can we take a look at your anxiety and see if we can help you with it?"*]

Role-Play Four

Th: Are you aware of feeling anxious?

Pt: Have you helped anyone like me before? [*"It sounds like you are wondering whether I can help you. Shall we pay attention to your anxiety and see if we can help you with it?"* The fact that the patient quickly changes subjects suggests that she may be anxious. Thus, addressing anxiety right away might be a good idea.*]*

Role-Play Five

Th: Are you aware of feeling anxious?

Pt: Yes, but I'm always anxious, and I think it's because of this show I saw last night. [*"If we come back to your anxiety, could we pay attention to your anxiety right now and see if we can help you with it?"*]

Role-Play Six

Th: Are you aware of feeling anxious?

Pt: There's always anxiety. That's just how I am. I've always been wired. [*"Wonderful that you notice. Could we pay attention to your anxiety right now and see if we can help you with it?"*]

Role-Play Seven

Th: Are you aware of feeling anxious?

Pt: I'm a little wired, sure, but that's because I just had two cups of coffee before I came here this morning. [*"So, could we take a look at how you experience this wiredness, this anxiety in your body right now, to see if we can bring it down?"*]

Role-Play Eight

Th: Are you aware of feeling anxious?

Pt: Not nervous, really. Just energized. I'm always going: go, go, go! [*"This energy is sometimes a sign of anxiety. Could we pay attention to your body right now and help you with your anxiety?"*]

Role-Play Nine

Th: Are you aware of feeling anxious?

Pt: I wouldn't say anxious. I'm afraid. I'm so afraid of what will happen if I relapse. [*"If we come back to this moment right now, could we pay attention to this anxiety in your body and see if we can help you bring it down?"*]

Role-Play Ten

Th: Are you aware of feeling anxious?

Pt: Wouldn't you be afraid, too, if your dealer said he was going to get you? [*"I'm sure I would. So, could we pay attention to this anxiety in your body and see if we can help you with it?"*]

Role-Play Eleven

Th: Are you aware of feeling anxious?

Pt: Yes, but I think it's because I'm going to the psychiatrist today, and I don't think he will renew my prescription for methadone. [*"If we come back to this moment right now, can we pay attention to this anxiety in your body and see if we can help you with it now?"*]

Pt: Yes. This is new for me. I'm not used to a therapist caring about my anxiety.

Very good! Notice how inviting the patient to pay attention to anxiety can block avoidance strategies and promote regulation. Help highly anxious patients focus on their anxiety as a first step in regulating it. Practice speaking slowly and calmly so that the patient can experience you as a safe haven.

As long as you block the ignoring strategy and invite the patient to pay attention to anxiety, your answer will be fine. The goal here is not to repeat the words in the book but to learn the principle guiding those words: block the ignoring of anxiety so the two of you can regulate it.

Now let's continue the role-play exercise. The person in the patient role should read the following to the person in the therapist role. "Let's do the exercise again. Whenever you intervene, I, as the patient, will go immediately to the next patient statement. Let's make this exercise feel like a real session. We won't stop for chitchat. We'll go straight through so you get the experience of processing and intervening more quickly. We'll repeat it several times. After you master this exercise, we'll shift roles so I can master it too."

Questions to ask each other to strengthen your skills: What do you notice feeling when you keep the focus on regulating your patient's anxiety? In the patient role, what did you experience as the therapist focused on regulating your anxiety? What did you learn from this experience that was new for you? What are you learning about the effects of ignoring anxiety as a habitual strategy? Did you experience your partner as criticizing your avoidance strategy or as caring about your anxiety? What advice might you offer your partner regarding slowness and calmness of speech? How are these exercises changing your previous understanding of the role of anxiety in therapy?

Skill-Building Exercise Six: Building the Capacity to Pay Attention to Anxiety

Principle: *Return the patient's attention to the physical experience of anxiety in the body to regulate it.*

Highly anxious patients often did not have someone pay careful attention to their anxiety, so they did not learn to do it. We have to help them develop that capacity in therapy. First, we help the patient notice her anxiety symptoms and identify them as anxiety. Then we build her capacity to pay attention to the physical sensations of anxiety in the body. The longer the patient can pay attention to a sensation in the body, the sooner her anxiety will come down. Also, the longer she can pay attention to her bodily sensations without acting out, the sooner she will develop impulse control. So, paying attention to anxiety is essential for anxiety regulation.

Exploring issues when the patient's anxiety is too high only triggers more anxiety, thus making therapy feel unsafe. If the patient doesn't feel safe, she will avoid exploring anything that triggers unregulated anxiety. We want to explore issues with patients only within a context of safety. Anxiety in the form of tension and sighing in the somatic nervous system indicates that the patient feels safe.

Practice a role-play exercise focused on helping the patient pay attention to her anxiety at HTRBook.com/Audio-6.

As the patient in this role-play exercise, read the following to your partner who is in the therapist role. "In the next role-play, which is much longer, I will play a patient who has trouble paying attention to my anxiety. Through many interventions, you will continue to focus on my anxiety, encouraging me to return my attention to my anxiety until it is regulated. This exercise will teach you how to persist until you have regulated my anxiety. And it will also teach you how to address different problems that come up when you try to help a patient regulate her anxiety. Now ask, 'Are you aware of feeling anxious?'"

> *Pt:* Before we get to that, can you give me medication? I'm really having trouble with withdrawal. [*"I can arrange for you to get medication if you need it. Since medication takes a while to have an effect, shall we take a look at your anxiety in your body now, and see if we can help you with it?"*]
>
> *Pt:* I guess so. [*"Where do you notice this anxiety physically in your body right now?"*]
>
> *Pt:* All over. [*"Okay. Good that you notice. Where do you notice feeling this anxiety in your body right now?"*]
>
> *Pt:* But I'm always anxious. [*"So, could we pay attention to your anxiety right now in your body and see if we can help you with it? Where do you notice feeling this anxiety in your body right now?"*]

Pt: I think it has to do with my being in withdrawal. [*"I wouldn't be surprised if that is part of the picture, so could we pay attention to your anxiety right now in your body and see if we can help you with it? Where do you notice feeling this anxiety in your body right now?"*]

Pt: I don't know. [*"Wouldn't it be nice to know? Could we pay attention to your anxiety right now and see if we can help you with it? Where do you notice feeling this anxiety in your body right now?"*]

Pt: I'm feeling sick to my stomach. [*"That's a sign of anxiety. What do you notice feeling there as you pay attention to this symptom in your stomach?"*]

Pt: Kind of nauseated. [*"Nausea is a sign of anxiety. As you notice that sensation in your stomach, is it getting bigger or smaller?"*]

Pt: I'm thinking I may get worse. [*"If we come back to this moment, could we shift your attention to this anxiety in your body? What do you notice feeling in your body as you keep your attention there?"*]

Pt: It feels like a ball down there. [*"Wonderful that you notice that. As you notice that ball, what changes happen in the ball as you notice it?"*]

Pt: It feels like it is pulsating. [*"Excellent that you notice that. What changes in the pulsating do you notice as you keep paying attention to those sensations?"*]

Pt: It feels like it is clenching. [*"Excellent you notice that. What changes in the clenching do you notice as you keep paying attention to it?" "Clenching" suggests that anxiety is shifting back into the somatic nervous system muscles. A good sign.*]

Pt: It feels like two things are happening: a pushing and a pulling. [*"Excellent that you notice that. What changes do you notice as you keep paying attention to the pushing and pulling?"*]

Pt: [*Sighs.*] I'm getting tense. [*"Wonderful. That's a sign your anxiety is coming down." The sigh and tension let us know that the patient's anxiety has shifted into the safe zone: the somatic nervous system. These are signs of regulated anxiety.*]

As long as you help the patient pay attention to anxiety so it can be regulated, your answers will be fine. The goal here is not to repeat the words in the book but to learn the principle guiding those words: help the patient pay attention to anxiety so it can be regulated.

Now let's continue the role-play exercise. The person in the patient role should read the following to the person in the therapist role. "Let's do the exercise again. Whenever you intervene, I, as the patient, will go immediately to the next patient statement. Let's make this exercise feel like a real session. We won't stop for chitchat. We'll go straight through so you get the experience of processing and intervening more quickly. We'll repeat it several times. After you master this exercise, we'll shift roles so I can master it too."

Questions to ask each other to strengthen your skills: What have you learned about anxiety that you did not know before doing these exercises? How does this new understanding change what you understood before? What are you paying attention to now that you didn't pay attention to before working on these skills? What new skills will you use to make therapy a safe place for the patient in the future? How are you becoming a safer person for the patient to depend upon? How did your partner change as an anxiety-regulating therapist?

You have just completed the first exercises on anxiety regulation. When patients begin therapy with excessive anxiety, we cannot establish a therapeutic alliance. We need to regulate anxiety so that the patient feels safe enough to declare a problem and work on it together with you.

CHAPTER FOUR

Developing the Right to Depend on Someone

When we ask a patient about the problem he would like us to help him with, we invite him to depend upon us. But what if in his past depending brought pain instead of relief? What if it was often unsafe for him to share his needs and problems? When the dangers of the past cast a shadow on the present, the patient's words may hide rather than reveal his problems. This happens automatically and unintentionally. Then he does not get the help he seeks. Thus, we must identify and block these avoidance strategies so the patient can share his problems and get the help he needs.

Principle for Avoidance Strategies:
> *Block avoidance strategies to invite a secure attachment.*

STAGE TWO: DECLARING A PROBLEM TO WORK ON

"What is the problem you would like me to help you with?" That seems like a simple question, doesn't it? But it's not just a factual question; it's a relational question: "Would you like to depend on me?" It's a difficult question for those whose parents told their children not to depend. "Quit bothering me!" "Stop whining!" "Shut up!"

If patients learned to hide their need for help in the past, they may avoid declaring a problem in therapy. It is nothing personal about you. Rather, impersonal, automatic rules guide the patients' relationships outside of their awareness. In response, we can block these learned strategies for hiding needs. Then we invite patients to reveal the problems they seek our help for.

Once patients can declare a problem to work on, we will have completed the first step in building a therapeutic alliance. Sometimes therapists do not establish a therapeutic alliance because they never found out the problem that motivated the patients to seek treatment. Find that problem.

Patients do not come to therapy saying, "Doctor, I want deeper insight into my conflicts." Patients come to therapy because they are suffering. So we need to find out the patient's problem.

Then we know what motivates him to seek therapy, and we can get a consensus on what we will do in therapy to resolve *his* problem to achieve *his* goals.

The following exercises will teach you how to help patients who have trouble declaring a problem to work on. Remember, when a patient does not declare a problem, he is not resisting therapy. He is collaborating according to the rule of the insecure attachment he grew up in: "Thou shalt not reveal a need."

HELPING WHEN PATIENTS DO NOT DECLARE A PROBLEM

To help a patient, the problem must first be identified. Practice the following exercise to learn how to get a patient to recognize the difference between a nonproblem and a real problem.

Skill-Building Exercise One: Offering Nonproblems Rather Than Real Problems

Fifty percent of patients leave therapy before receiving the full benefit, and if patients don't improve within the first seven sessions, they aren't likely to get better (Wierzbidki and Pekorik l993). Why don't they improve? They don't form an effective therapeutic alliance. To form any good working alliance, partners must agree on what they will do and why they will do it (Bordin 1994). The problem is the reason the patient comes to therapy. That's why both the therapist and patient must agree on the problem the patient wants to resolve.

When patients have trouble declaring a problem to work on, they may offer a nonproblem instead of a real problem. For instance, the patient might present something that sounds like a problem for someone else but not for the patient. Do not explore any issue, no matter how severe, if the patient does not regard it as a problem. If she does not consider it a problem, she has no motivation to explore it. Here's an example:

Th: What is the problem you would like me to help you with?

Pt: I'm living with my husband, but he's just a placeholder for now until I leave.

Th: Is that a problem you would like me to help you with?

Pt: No. I'm fine with it.

Th: Okay. Since that's not a problem for you, what is the problem you would like me to help you with?

Do not argue with the patient. In therapy, we explore what *she* thinks is a problem, not what we think is a problem. If she regards something as not a problem, we have no right to explore it. In fact, our respect for her wish not to explore an issue often mobilizes her desire to explore it.

When patients present a nonproblem, you can respond by saying, "It's not clear how that is a problem for you. So, what is the problem you'd like me to help you with?" If they maintain that everything is fine, you can respond, "Great! Yet, if everything were fine, you wouldn't be here. So, I wonder: what the problem is you would like me to help you with?"

Practice blocking nonproblems and returning the focus to real problems at HTRBook.com /Audio-7.

As the patient in this role-play exercise, read the following to your partner who is in the therapist role. "I will play a patient who responds with nonproblems. Block my nonproblem and return the focus to an internal problem. After you answer, I'll give you the recommended answer. Don't worry if your words are not identical to those in the book. As long as you block the avoidance strategy and return the focus to the problem, your answers will be fine. The goal here is not to repeat the words in the book but to learn the principle guiding those words: block a nonproblem and return to the focus on an internal problem.

"Here you will learn how to block misalliance behaviors to promote a therapeutic alliance. Now we will begin the role-play exercise. Ask me, 'What is the problem you want me to help you with?'"

> Pt: My kids are doing well, my job is great, and overall everything is going just fine. [*"That's wonderful. But if everything were going wonderfully, you wouldn't be here. So, what is the problem you'd like me to help you with?"*]
>
> Pt: I want my kids to do better in school, and I was hoping you could help me help them. [*"I hear that your kids have a problem at school. But it's not clear how that is an internal problem for you. So, what is your problem that you would like me to help you with?"*]
>
> Pt: I don't know. [*"And yet you are here. So, what is the problem you would like me to help you with?"*]
>
> Pt: My wife and I have been in couples' therapy, and the couples therapist recommended I see you since the literature shows, she said, that couples therapy plus individual therapy is the best combination. [*"This is what your therapist said, but it is not clear what the problem is you would like me to help you with. What is the problem you would like me to help you with?"*]
>
> Pt: The human resources people also recommended I see you. I'm a high-level executive. I'm very successful and good at what I do. I'm the person they send in to close the deal because they know I'm very good with people. [*"That's great, so can you be more specific about what you want me to help you with?"*]
>
> Pt: My ex-girlfriend said I should see a therapist. I told her about the affair I'm having, and she really reamed me out over that. [*Rolls his eyes.*] She thinks I shouldn't be unfaithful to my wife. She's probably right. But you know I've been having affairs in my marriage for twenty years. It's a great way to be sexually satisfied, and women are always hitting on me, eager to hop into bed. Who am I to say no? [*"You say it's a problem for your ex-girlfriend, but it's not clear how this is a problem for you. What is the problem you would like me to help you with?"*]

Pt: I'm an adult child of an alcoholic, and I've been reading a lot of books about that. My father and mother were both drinkers. And, from what I've read, it's clear that what parents do to you influences your adult life. [*"Before we go into your history, could you be more specific about what your problem is today that you want me to help you with?"*]

Pt: I wondered if my wife had been having an affair. She denied it and denied it. But then, about two weeks ago, just before I called you, she told me she had had an affair. So, anyway, we have talked about it and thought the most logical solution would be for us to divorce. She would take the kids and move to New Jersey, and I would stay here and have the kids with me two months a year. [*"You mention the affairs and the solution of divorce and childcare arrangements. But it's still not clear how this is an internal emotional problem for you. What is the problem you want me to help you with?"*]

Pt: I'm not sure what to work on. I hadn't thought of anything. I suppose we could talk about my drug use. But to be honest, it's not a big deal for me. [*"Since the drug use is not a big deal for you, what is the internal problem you would like me to help you with."*]

Pt: My wife is very controlling. We have been in marital therapy for years but with no result. She is still controlling. I have tried talking to her about it, but it doesn't do any good. [*"You have described your wife, but it's not clear how this is an internal emotional problem for you. Could you be more specific about the internal emotional problem you would like me to help you with?"*]

Pt: She said that if I don't start treating her better, I have to move out. [*"And is this pattern with your wife the problem you want us to work on together?"*]

Pt: [*Sighs.*] Yes, because I don't want to lose her and the kids.

When patients avoid declaring a problem quickly, they don't sit around thinking, "Hmm, which avoidance strategy should I use?" They avoid automatically. They don't even know they are avoiding. When you block these strategies as rapidly as they come up, the patient will soon offer a problem and get the help he needs.

Now let's continue the role-play exercise. The person in the patient role should read the following to the person in the therapist role. "Let's do the exercise again. Whenever you intervene, I, as the patient, will go immediately to the next patient statement. Let's make this exercise feel like a real session. We won't stop for chitchat. We'll go straight through so you get the experience of processing and intervening more quickly. We'll repeat it several times. After you master this exercise, we'll shift roles so I can master it too. As long as you block the avoidance strategy and return the focus to the problem, your answer will be fine. The goal here is not to repeat the words in the book but to learn the principle guiding those words: block a nonproblem and return to the focus on an internal problem."

Questions to ask each other to strengthen your skills: After doing this skill-building exercise, how would you differentiate an internal emotional problem from a nonproblem? How does recognizing a nonproblem change your understanding of the patient's conflict about depending? How does recognizing a nonproblem change your understanding about what we mean by a therapeutic focus? What did you learn through the therapist's clear therapeutic focus when you were in the patient role? What did you experience when your partner blocked avoidance strategies? What advice might you give your partner? What is like for you to see avoidance strategies that the patient cannot see? How does this change your understanding of the patient when you see how automatic strategies can occur outside the patient's awareness?

After you do this exercise, watch HTRBook.com/Video-8 for a review.

THEORETICAL INTERLUDE: THE RELATIONAL ISSUES THAT A THERAPEUTIC ALLIANCE TRIGGERS

Many patients can tell you the problem they want help with. But some patients want your help and then don't reveal their problem. What a surprise! Why does that happen? When we relate to the patient, his relational history may arise in the form of insecure attachment behaviors. So, let's examine how co-creating a therapeutic alliance brings out the patient's relational problems.

Take, for example, the question: "What is the problem you would like me to help you with?" On the one hand, it seems like a simple enough question. But for the patient, your question means: "You are asking me to depend on you, but when I depended before, I was hurt, abused, and abandoned." Sometimes parents told our patients that they should not have problems or need help. They learned, "Do not ask for help!" And Yet, you invite them to ask. No wonder these patients have trouble answering that question.

They are actually collaborating with you when they avoid declaring a problem to work on. They are telling you: "I have learned to hide a problem to keep a relationship." Perfect! You may need to help the patient for five or twenty minutes with the ways he avoids declaring a problem until he declares one. While doing that, you won't be working toward a supposedly "right" answer. Instead, you will be helping the patient overcome his fear of depending on people. And that problem must get worked out with you so he can form a therapeutic alliance. So, what if it takes twenty minutes until he declares a problem?

When doing relational work, we can get focused on getting a "better" answer rather than building a better relationship. The patient may not give you the answer you want, but he always gives you the one you need. Find out why his answer is perfect. We need to know what his problem is. But his avoidance strategies reveal that he is afraid to reveal a problem. He enacts his problem perfectly.

Pt: I don't have a problem.

Th: And Yet, you are here. And I'm sure an intelligent man like you wouldn't come here for no reason at all. So, what is the problem you would like me to help you with?

His response is not an obstacle; it reveals his issue: "I am not supposed to have problems or to depend on people. In my early insecure attachment, I learned that I could have a problem or a relationship. Since I couldn't have both, I hid my problems to keep a relationship."

Persistently invite a secure attachment as he tests you to determine whether you will accept his need to depend without judging him. You will not pass this test after one question. Instead, your persistent and patient focus on his problem will demonstrate to him that you accept him *and* his problem. Your unwavering, supportive focus shows that you believe he has the right to declare a problem and ask for help.

When you stop focusing on getting the right answer from your fantasy patient, you will start building an alliance with the real patient you have. Don't focus on the responses you want. Focus on the relationship. If you focus on the answers you want, the patient will realize that you want "right" answers instead of real responses. He will realize that you want a fantasy person rather than a real relationship with him, and a misalliance will develop.

As you persist in finding out the patient's problem, he may mistakenly think you want something from him. Remind him of reality: he came to you because *he* wants something from therapy. To help him, we need to know the problem *he* wants help with. Otherwise, he will not get the help he needs. His reluctance does not conflict with *your* desire. His reluctance conflicts with *his* desire for help. His reluctance holds him back. To help him with his problem, we need to know what it is. This stance has nothing to do with a particular model of therapy. It's just how reality works.

But as you persist and focus on his problem, the patient may become anxious. Are you doing something wrong? No. Anxiety means that you are focusing on the central relationship issue: depending on another person. Notice that I didn't write "depending on you." Why? When a patient has trouble depending on a therapist, he usually has trouble depending on anyone. That's why he gets anxious: he is going into new territory—admitting that he needs help and wants to depend. Thus, when you focus on his problem, you not only help the patient develop a therapeutic alliance, you help him improve all of his relationships.

To understand the relational context of our interventions, look at the sequence of interventions therapists offer and the relational issues they trigger in patients.

Intervention: What is the problem you would like me to help you with?
Relational issue for the patient: "Do I have the right to have a problem in a relationship?" "Do I have the right to depend in a relationship?" "Will you judge, punish, or abandon me if I depend upon you?"
Intervention: Is it your will to work on this problem?
Relational issue for the patient: "Do I have the right to say no?" "Do I have the right to have a separate will?" "Do I have the right to a relationship based on my agenda rather than submitting to your agenda?"
Intervention: Would it make sense to focus on this conflict you have with your husband so we could help you assert yourself more effectively?

Relational issue for the patient: "Do I have the right to set the goals we will work toward?" "Do I have the right to co-create this relationship for change?" "Will you judge, punish, or abandon me if I assert myself as an equal partner?"

Intervention: What would be a specific example of this problem you would like us to focus on?

Relational issue for the patient: "Do I have permission to explore my issues with you?" "Do you *really* want to know me?" "May I depend on you, and do you really want to focus on my problems to help me?" "In the past, the people who were supposed to help me hurt me. Will you do the same?"

Intervention: What feelings did you have toward him when he did that?

Relational issue for the patient: "Do I have the right to have feelings?" "Do I have the right to focus on my feelings with you?" "Will you judge, punish, or abandon me if I reveal my feelings?"

Avoidance strategies previously preserved the patient's relationships. Today they corrupt her connections. They solved a problem in the past, but they produce her problems in the present. We help her let go of these outdated strategies so she can present a problem and work on it with you. Through this new experience, we co-create a secure attachment, opening a pathway toward better relationships with others. Patients seek help but fear they will be hurt. They have a need but fear to reveal it: a need-fear dilemma (Burnham, Gladstone, and Gibson 1969).

See how to validate the patient's need instead of her avoidance strategies at HTRBook.com /Video-9.

Every intervention offering a secure attachment will trigger relational issues for the patient. The patient responds not just to your intervention but *to the relationship you are inviting*. Now you can see the true purpose of your work. You do not intervene to get the right answer. That so-called right answer is just the answer you want. If you want the patient to give you *your* answer, you are no longer interested in *her* answer. Yet her response is always right. Her answer tells you the problem she has now in forming an alliance. Help her with those problems so you can co-create a therapeutic alliance.

A therapeutic alliance is not any kind of relationship. For instance, a passive, compliant relationship is a relationship. In therapy, we co-create a *working* relationship. We *work together* on a *therapeutic task* to achieve the *patient's* positive goals. And the task must be one that the patient and therapist have agreed upon.

Therapy can't be based on the therapist's goals because it is the patient's therapy. Thus, we design the therapy to achieve the patient's positive goals. Only the positive goals that *she* desires will motivate her to do the hard work of therapy.

The following exercises will teach you skills for helping patients who have a hard time telling you the problem that brings them to your office.

See how to respond to clients who are not stating their problems at HTRBook.com/Video-10.

Skill-Building Exercise Two: Changing Topics to Avoid Declaring a Problem

Sometimes when you ask a patient about her problem, she will shift to a different topic. This is how she protected others from her need to depend. She does it with you automatically and unintentionally, without even knowing it happened. When that happens, block that shift away from the problem, and return to the problem.

For instance, if the therapist asks, "What is the problem you would like me to help you with?" the patient may respond by saying, "Gosh, you have nice hair. Who is your hairdresser?" She changed the topic. In response, block the new topic and return to the problem: "Thanks. Coming back to my question, what is the problem you would like me to help you with?"

Or suppose you ask, "What is the problem you would like me to help you with?" The patient might say, "I think there's a lot of history I need to tell you about my childhood." Here you can say, "I'm sure there is. But first, what is the problem you would like me to help you with?" Here, history came up, not the problem she wants your help with.

See how to help patients who change topics to avoid talking about the problem at HTRBook.com /Video-11.

Practice a role-play exercise to help the patient return to the problem at HTRBook.com/Audio-8.

As the patient in this role-play exercise, read the following to your partner who is in the therapist role. "As before, you will ask: 'What is the problem you would like me to help you with?' and I will be your patient. I will offer a problem, or I will change topics. If I respond with a problem, explore it. If I change topics, block the avoidance strategy of changing topics and return to the problem. Now we will do the role-play exercise. Go ahead ask me, 'What is the problem you would like me to help you with?'"

Pt: Let me tell you about what happened last night because I think it is related. [*"Before we get to that, what is the problem you would like me to help you with?"*]

Pt: I think there's a whole lot of history I need to tell you about my childhood. [*"And we can look at that. But first, what is the problem you would like me to help you with?"*]

Pt: This is a nice office. [*"Thanks. Coming back to your problem, what is the problem you would like me to help you with?"*]

Pt: My friends say I should leave my husband. [*"That's what your friends say. But, in your opinion, what is the problem you would like me to help you with?"*]

Pt: Boy, it was hard to park today. Is it always so busy on your street? [*"Sometimes it is. Coming back to your problem, what is the problem you would like me to help you with?"*]

Pt: It's a beautiful day today. [*"Yes, it is. And coming back here, what is the problem you would like me to help you with?"*]

Pt: Oh, what a day it has been. I just got here from the hairdresser's, and then after this, I rush to my dermatologist to have my skin moisturized. . . . [*"If we leave the doctors in the waiting room, what is the emotional problem you would like me to help you with?"*]

Pt: Did anyone ever tell you that you have beautiful eyes? [*"Thank you. Coming back to your problem, what is the problem you would like me to help you with?"*]

Pt: I was in rehab before, but it didn't do much good. I didn't care for the place. [*"I hear that rehab didn't do much good. To make sure we do some good this time, what is the problem you would like me to help you with?"*]

Pt: Let me tell you about what I just saw out on the sidewalk. There was the cutest child with his mother, and she gave him an ice cream cone. [*"If we leave them on the sidewalk, what is the problem you would like me to help you with here?"*]

Pt: Well, let me tell you about what happened on Saturday. [*"Before we do that, right now, today, what is the problem you would like me to help you with?"*]

Pt: The first thing I should probably tell you is that I first started using drugs when I was thirteen years old. [*"Before we go into your history, what is the problem you would like me to help you with?"*]

Pt: The usual childhood issues. Sexual abuse. Trauma. You know. [*"And now? What is the problem now you would like me to help you with?"*]

Pt: Could you tell me how your therapy works? [*"You'll see how the therapy works just from your experience here today with me. So, could we look at the problem you would like me to help you with?"*]

Pt: Did the intake person tell you about the things we had discussed? [*"Only a little. So, in your own words, what is the problem you would like me to help you with?"*]

Pt: I suppose this is a question you therapists always ask. [*"Sure. If we know what the problem is you want help with, we can make sure therapy helps you with your problem. So, what is the problem you would like me to help you with?"*]

Pt: I have some ideas about it. [*"So, what is the problem you would like me to help you with?"*]

Pt: I got raped on a date about a month ago, and it really freaked me out. And I've been using drugs ever since, and I can't seem to stop. [*"No wonder you came. Would you like us to see what got triggered so we can help you deal with these feelings in a different way than by using drugs?"*]

Now let's continue the role-play exercise. The person in the patient role should read the following to the person in the therapist role. "Let's do the exercise again. Each time you intervene, I, as the patient, will go immediately to the next patient statement. Let's make this exercise feel like a real session. We won't stop to chat. Instead, we'll go straight through so you, the therapist, get the experience of processing and intervening more quickly. We'll repeat this until you have mastered it. Then we'll change roles and do it again until I master it too. As long as you block the avoidance strategy and return the focus to the problem, your answer will be fine. The goal here is not to repeat the words in the book but to learn the principle guiding those words: block the avoidance strategy and focus again on the problem."

Questions to ask each other to strengthen your skills: What do you understand about changing topics that you did not understand before this exercise? What impact does changing topics have on maintaining a therapeutic focus? When you were in the patient role, what did you experience and learn when the therapist maintained a therapeutic focus? How did you experience your therapist when the avoidance strategy was getting blocked? What advice might you offer your partner to create a caring environment? Did you interrupt the patient or did you interrupt the strategies that were interrupting her, preventing her from revealing her problem? How does this change your previous understanding of your role in therapy?

Skill-Building Exercise Three: Offering Vague Answers to Avoid Declaring a Problem

Sometimes when you ask for the patient's problem, he will respond so vaguely you don't know what he wants to work on. Often, patients learned to use vagueness to hide their problems and needs from caretakers. Vagueness was a way to become invisible. Unfortunately, that automatic response can happen in therapy too. So, again, we will block his avoidance strategy and invite him to depend upon us in a secure attachment.

When the patient responds with vagueness, point out the vagueness and then invite him to be more specific about the problem. For instance, suppose you ask, "What is the problem you would like me to help you with?"

> *Pt:* A variety of problems. Well, maybe not problems, issues might be a better word.
>
> *Th:* Issues is vague. [*Labeling the avoidance strategy.*] Could you be more specific about the problem you would like me to help you with? [*Returning the focus to the problem.*]

Patients don't intend to be vague. They aren't even aware of the vagueness. To help them see it, help them see they are being vague by repeating their vague words. Then they'll understand what you are talking about. In the previous example, we could have said, "'variety of problems' is vague." Now the patient knows what words were vague. Then you can invite him to be more specific.

See how to help patients who use vagueness to avoid declaring a problem to work on at HTRBook .com/Video-12.

Practice dealing with the avoidance strategy of vagueness at HTRBook.com/Audio-9.

As the patient in this role-play exercise, read the following to your partner who is in the therapist role. "I will play the role of the patient. You will ask about the problem I want help with, but my responses will be vague. Repeat the vague words, point out the vagueness, and invite me to be more specific about the problem I want your help for. Begin the role-play by asking me, 'What is the problem you would like me to help you with?'"

> *Pt:* Well, I think it has to do with things that happened in my childhood. [*"Things is vague. Could you be more specific about the problem you would like me to help you with?"*]

Pt: There has been a lot of bad stuff happening. [*"Bad stuff is vague. Could you be more specific about the internal problem you would like me to help you with?"*]

Pt: I think the problem has to do with upset feelings over recent events. [*"Upset feelings is vague. Could you be more specific about the internal problem you would like me to help you with?"*]

Pt: A bad situation. [*"Bad situation is vague. Could you be more specific about the internal problem you would like me to help you with?"*]

Pt: I feel upset about things. [*"Upset about things is vague. Could you be more specific about the internal problem you would like me to help you with?"*]

Pt: I'm bummed out. [*"Bummed out is vague. Could you be more specific about the internal problem you would like me to help you with?"*]

Pt: It's been really hot lately. We've been tired, and things have been hard. [*"Things have been hard is vague. Could you be more specific about the internal problem you would like me to help you with?"*]

Pt: Dissatisfaction with how things are going. [*"Dissatisfaction is vague. Could you be more specific about the internal problem you would like me to help you with?"*]

Pt: There's been some disagreement about things and tension about that. [*"Disagreement is vague. Could you be more specific about the internal problem you would like me to help you with?"*]

Pt: I've been feeling out of sorts lately about things that have been going on. [*"Out of sorts is vague. Could you be more specific about the internal problem that you would like me to help you with?"*]

Pt: Uncertainty about the future with my wife. [*"Uncertainty is vague. Could you be more specific about the problem you would like me to help you with?"*]

Pt: I've been wondering about my future, my past, everything really. [*"Wondering is vague. Could you be more specific about the internal problem you would like me to help you with?"*]

Pt: I feel a stone in my stomach. [*"A stone in the stomach is vague. Could you be more specific about the internal emotional problem you would like me to help you with?"*]

Pt: Things have not been going so well. Not so happy with the way my life is going. [*"Not so happy is vague. Could you be more specific about the internal emotional problem you would like me to help you with?"*]

Pt: I feel uneasy. [*"Uneasy is vague. Could you be more specific about the emotional problem you would like me to help you with?"*]

Pt: I can't seem to hold a job. I just got put on probation. And if I don't get a handle on this, I'm afraid I'm going to get fired again. [*"And would you like us to see if we can find out what is causing this problem with jobs so you could be more successful?" In this example, the patient offered a clear example of a problem.*]

Now let's continue the role-play exercise. The person in the patient role should read the following to the person in the therapist role. "Now we'll repeat the exercise. As soon as you, the therapist, intervene, I, the patient, will go immediately to the next patient statement. Let's make this exercise

feel like a real session. We won't stop to talk about the exercise. Instead, we'll go straight through so you, the therapist, get the experience of processing and intervening more quickly. We'll repeat this until you have mastered it. Then we'll change roles and do it again until I have mastered it too. As long as you block the avoidance strategy and return the focus to the problem, your answer will be fine. The goal here is not to repeat the words in the book but to learn the principle guiding those words: label the vagueness and focus again on the problem."

Questions to ask each other to strengthen your skills: What do you understand about vagueness that you did not understand before you did this exercise? What was the hardest part about learning to identify vagueness? What did you experience and learn when the therapist kept a therapeutic focus? What were forms of vagueness you learned about here that you used to hear but not address with patients? What impact has patients' vagueness had on your previous therapies? Was your partner able to talk about vagueness in a nonjudgmental way? How might your partner convey acceptance rather than judgment of the patient's avoidance strategies? Did you interrupt the patient or did the vagueness interrupt the patient, preventing him from telling his problem? How might you describe vagueness rather than criticize it? How might your tone of voice change? How could you do that now so your partner can listen and assess your stance?

A Theoretical Interlude: Aren't You Interrupting the Patient?

As we go through these exercises, you may wonder, "Aren't I interrupting the patient?" We never interrupt the patient. We interrupt the avoidance strategies that interrupt the patient. She wants help. But her avoidance strategies don't let her get it. They constantly interrupt her, so she can't share her problem. *That's why we never interrupt the patient. To show our compassion for her, we interrupt the avoidance strategies that are interrupting and hurting her.* Then she can reveal her problem.

"But aren't we supposed to listen?" you ask. Absolutely! We listen to the patient, but we block the interrupters that prevent her from listening to her need. If interrupters keep coming up, they will distract her, preventing her from sharing the problem for which she wants our help.

Let's dig a little further into this question of listening. Remember how we talked earlier about conflict? The patient wants one thing, but automatic behaviors give her something else. She tries to talk about her problem, and automatic avoidance strategies take her off topic. As soon as she talks about something important, avoidance strategies take her off track. We listen carefully and then block the interrupters that get in the patient's way. Otherwise, the interrupters prevent her from getting the help she needs. For instance, we learned how nonproblems or vagueness prevented the patient from sharing a problem. They interrupted her outside of her awareness. That's why we block those interrupters. If we block them enough, they can't keep the patient from sharing her problem.

Always listen to the patient, and help her see the interrupters that get in her way. Then she gains the ability to talk freely about her problems without these habitual interrupters blocking her. But learning to listen to the patient while addressing avoidance strategies is a new and foreign skill for therapists. Why?

As children, we learned to accept and even strengthen other people's avoidance strategies. Remember when Uncle Ed said something awkward, and mother stood up suddenly and said, "Okay everyone, time to go to the dining room for dinner? Mother provided an avoidance strategy. We consider those good manners. To be polite, we accept and strengthen avoidance in others. For instance, when someone has lost a parent, socialization has prepared us to say, "Are you okay?" And socialization has prepared our relatives to say, "I'm fine." We consider that polite behavior.

But in therapy, we do not support avoidance strategies that cause the patient's symptoms and suffering. Instead, we point out avoidance strategies that we previously passed over in silence, and we block those strategies so the patient can finally tell us where she wants help.

That's why therapy can initially feel uncomfortable for therapists. We are going against a lifetime of socialization where we supported avoidance strategies. But if we support the patient's avoidance strategies, we will help her avoid what she needs to face. And her symptoms will not improve. That's why, as therapists, we do not support avoidance strategies; we support the patient instead.

See how to help patients who offer a thought instead of their problem at HTRBook.com/Video-13.

By herself, the patient had to avoid what was too much. Alone, she had to rely on an avoidance strategy. But in the therapeutic relationship, she can depend on you. Then the two of you can face together what she could not face by herself.

Rather than facilitate avoidance strategies, therapists block those strategies to form a therapeutic alliance. Then we encourage patients to face what makes them anxious so they can master their fears. With your courage and help blocking the interrupters, patients can find the courage in therapy to face with you what they previously had to avoid when alone.

To make this shift, we help patients see avoidance strategies. An avoidance strategy is any maladaptive behavior or thought that hurts the patient. Let's look at the next avoidance strategy so you can get better at listening to the patient and blocking her interrupters. Blocking the interrupters is one way we show compassion for the patient and support her wish for help.

Skill-Building Exercise Four: Offering Thoughts Rather Than a Problem to Work On

When you ask the patient for his problem, he may offer thoughts instead of the problem. For instance, you ask, "What's the problem you would like me to help you with?"

Pt: "I think my issues here are emotional ones or maybe not emotional but behavioral problems."

Th: "That's your thought. But what is the problem you would like me to help you with?"

The patient offers thoughts while observing the taboo against depending. "Don't worry, Mom. I won't depend on you. I'll offer thoughts instead. Do you feel comfortable now?" "If I show you my head instead of my heart, can you love me now?"

Sometimes, instead of giving a problem, the patient will say, "I have this problem *because* of my boss." The word "because" is a sign of rationalization. The patient tells you the reason for his problem, not the problem itself. Block the rationalization, and return to the focus. "That may be the reason for your problem, but what is the problem itself you would like me to help you with?"

See how to help patients declare their problems at HTRBook.com/Video-14.

Practice returning the patient's focus to the problem at HTRBook.com/Audio-10.

As the patient in this role-play exercise, read the following to your partner who is in the therapist role. "In this role-play, I will play a patient who offers thoughts instead of a problem. Or I will offer reasons for the problem but not the problem itself. Block the avoidance strategy and return to the focus on my problem. Begin the role-play exercise by asking me, 'What is the problem you would like me to help you with?'"

Pt: The reason I am seeing you is probably due to my early upbringing. ["*That may be the reason for your problem, but what is the problem you would like me to help you with?*"]

Pt: My previous rehab said I have a passive-aggressive personality, and that may be a problem. ["*That was their idea. If we come back to you, what is the problem you would like me to help you with?*"]

Pt: I'm here due to a midlife crisis. I am wondering about the meaning of my life and where my marriage is going. ["*These are among the reasons you are here, but what is the internal emotional problem you would like me to help you with?*" *Emphasize an internal emotional problem so he won't continue to ruminate about external problems.*]

Pt: I have been trying to figure that out, and so I have written a list of thoughts I have about this for you to read. Would you like to read it now? ["*These are some thoughts you have about your problem, but first, could you be more specific about the problem itself that you would like me to help you with?*"]

Pt: Could I tell you about what I learned from working through *A Course in Miracles*? ["*Before we go to your thoughts about that book, could you be more specific about the problem itself that you would like me to help you with?*"]

Pt: I had a good experience with my last therapist, and I thought I would like to have that kind of help again. ["*Thank you for sharing your thought. Could you be more specific about what you want me to help you with in this therapy?*"]

Pt: I don't understand what you mean by problem. Perhaps you could explain to me what that means, and then I might be able to answer your question. ["*Just the problem you would like me to help you with.*" *Sometimes therapists wonder, "What if he really doesn't understand?" Asking what the problem is is a simple question. The patient who "doesn't understand" is hiding his problem. He probably hides in other relationships the same way. If the patient insists he does not*] *understand, you can remind the patient of reality: "Insofar as you have come to me, a therapist, to help you with a psychological problem, naturally, I'm wondering what the problem is that you would like me to help you with. Obviously, if we don't find out what your problem is, we won't be able to help you with it. So, what is the problem you want my help with?"]*

Pt: I've got some problems. I don't know if they have anything to do with drugs. [*"This is your thought about your problems. What is the problem itself for which you want my help?"*]

Pt: I think I've got a lot of abuse issues from my childhood. [*"These may be reasons for your problem, but what is the internal problem today for which you want my help?"*]

Pt: Boy. You are persistent! I guess I'll tell you what I didn't tell my previous therapist. I've been wanting to kill myself. [*"When did you start having those thoughts?" In this last exchange, the patient offered a clear problem, so the therapist asks about the event that triggered this suicidal ideation.*]

Offering thoughts or reasons instead of a problem is very common. As long as you block the avoidance strategy and return the focus to the problem, your answer will be fine. The goal here is not to repeat the words in the book but to learn the principle guiding those words: block the thought about the problem or the reason for it and return the focus to the problem.

Now let's continue the role-play exercise. The person in the patient role should read the following to the person in the therapist role. "Now we'll repeat the exercise. As soon as you, the therapist, intervene, I, the patient, will go immediately to the next patient statement. Let's make this exercise feel like a real session. We won't stop to chat during the exercise. Instead, we'll go straight through so you, the therapist, get the experience of processing and intervening more quickly. We'll repeat this until you have mastered it. Then we'll change roles and do it again until I have mastered it too."

Questions to ask each other to strengthen your skills: What do you understand about the difference between thoughts and a problem that you did not understand before this exercise? How will this change affect your work? Insofar as thoughts prevented the patient from offering a problem, what do you understand now about the patient's conflict around depending upon you? In the patient role, what did you experience and understand about the difference between thoughts and a problem? How did you feel as you experienced the therapist's persistence in finding out where you wanted help? How did you experience your therapist in this role-play? How could your partner convey acceptance rather than judgment of the patient's avoidance strategies? How is your recognition of avoidance strategies changing how you understand the patient's statements?

Skill-Building Exercise Five: Helping Patients Who Say That Someone Else Thinks They Should Be in Therapy

Sometimes when you ask the patient about his problem, he says he doesn't think he has one. His wife thinks he does. Since the patient has not declared what *he* thinks is a problem, we have no right to do therapy yet. Instead, you can respond, "Since your wife is not here, I can't help her. So, I wonder, what is the internal problem *you* would like me to help you with?"

Again, notice how the patient obeys the rules of an insecure attachment. "Don't worry, Dad. I know the rules: no depending. Someone else thought I should depend." The patient does not use this avoidance strategy consciously or intentionally. It happens automatically outside of his awareness.

And since he has not Yet, declared a problem, we have no right to do therapy Yet, by commenting on his avoidance strategies. That's why we block them and return to the focus on a problem. If you comment on his avoidance strategies before he has declared a problem and a desire to do therapy, he can feel easily accused, and you will get into a misalliance with the patient. So, in this initial phase, do not comment on his avoidance strategies. Just block them and return to the focus on a problem. He must first declare a problem and his will to work on it before we have permission to explore anything in therapy.

Watch a demonstration of working with patients who say someone else thinks they need therapy at HTRBook.com/Video-15.

Practice working with a patient who doesn't declare a problem at HTRBook.com/Audio-11.

As the patient in this role-play exercise, read the following to your partner who is in the therapist role. "In this role-play exercise, I will play a patient who doesn't declare a problem and instead says that someone thinks therapy would be a good idea. Remind me of reality and return to the problem. Begin the role-play exercise by asking me, 'What is the problem you would like me to help you with?'"

> *Pt:* My doctor sent me here. [*"Since your doctor is not here, I can't help him. So, what is the problem you would like me to help you with?"*]
>
> *Pt:* My boss told me I have to come here. [*"Since your boss is not here, I can't help him. So, what is the problem you would like me to help you with?"*]
>
> *Pt:* My husband thinks I have a problem with intimacy. [*"That is what your husband thinks, but, in your opinion, what is the problem you want me to help you with?"*]
>
> *Pt:* My sponsor said I am passive-aggressive. [*"That's what your sponsor thinks, but in your opinion, what is the problem you would like me to help you with?"*]
>
> *Pt:* My husband said that I need to be in therapy because I have an anger problem. [*"That's his opinion. But in your opinion, what is the problem you would like me to help you with?"*]
>
> *Pt:* He thinks if I'm in therapy, our marriage might get better. [*"That's his opinion of what you need, but what is the problem that you want help with for yourself here?"*]
>
> *Pt:* He thinks I have a problem with drugs. [*"That's his opinion. What's yours? What is the problem you would like me to help you with?"*]
>
> *Pt:* I have to come here if I want to keep my job. [*"That still doesn't tell us though what the problem is you would like help with. What is the problem you would like me to help you with?"*]

Pt: I don't know. You'll have to ask my boss. He's the one who put me on probation. [*"But this can't be his therapy. For this to be your therapy to achieve your goals, what is the problem you would like me to help you with?"*]

Pt: I guess the drug use because if I don't deal with that, I'm going to lose my job. [*"I hear that the drug use is a problem for your workplace. But is the drug use a problem for you that you want us to focus on here for your benefit?" Do not assume his drug use is the problem he wants to work on. Ask to make sure.*]

Pt: [*Sighs.*] Yes, because I can't afford to lose this job.

Now we'll repeat the exercise. As long as you block the avoidance strategy and return the focus to the problem, your answer will be fine. The goal here is not to repeat the words in the book but to learn the principle guiding those words: remind the patient of reality and ask if this is the problem he wants to work on.

Now let's continue the role-play exercise. The person in the patient role should read the following to the person in the therapist role. "As soon as you, the therapist, intervene, I, the patient, will go immediately to the next patient statement. Let's make this exercise feel like a real session. We won't stop for talking. We'll go straight through so you, the therapist, get the experience of processing and intervening more quickly. We'll repeat this until you have mastered it. Then we'll change roles and do it again until I have mastered it too."

An Additional Example

The patient's desire must drive therapy, not others' desires. In this short example, I will start the role-play by playing a patient who has come to therapy as a condition of his parole.

Pt: I have to be here as a condition of my parole. [*"But that still doesn't say what you want me to help you with."*]

Pt: I don't have a problem. I have to be here because I'm required as part of my parole. [*"I realize you may have to be in therapy, but I don't have to do therapy. It may be that you have no problem. And if so, there is no reason for us to meet. After all, why should you waste your time pretending to do therapy when you don't have a problem? And why should I pretend to help someone who doesn't need it?"*]

Pt: But I have to do it because of parole! [*"I realize you may have to pretend to do therapy when you have no problem. But I don't have to pretend to do therapy with someone who doesn't have a problem. That would be a waste of our time."*]

Repeat this brief exercise several times until you master it. This is a challenging Yet, essential skill when working with mandated patients. In this exercise, you set a limit with the patient, letting him know that your integrity is not for sale. This intervention may lead the patient to begin an honest therapy for himself rather than a pretend therapy for his parole officer.

Questions to ask each other to strengthen your skills: What did you learn about this strategy ("Other people say I should be in therapy") that you did not know before doing this skill-building exercise? What did you notice feeling as you focused on the patient's will rather than the will of others? In the patient role, what did you feel when you could not distract the therapist from what *you* thought was your problem? What did you learn when you were in the patient role? What did you feel when you held onto your integrity, your therapist role? What did you learn by holding onto your therapist role that was new for you? What was the hardest part of holding onto the therapist role? In the patient role, what did you feel when the therapist held onto the therapist role? What did you learn in the patient role that was new for you? In the last example, were you able to describe the patient's situation in a concerned, factual manner, or did you slip into being judgmental? How might you shift into a noncritical stance when you do that role-play again?

A Theoretical Interlude: Getting Frustrated Yet?

You want to establish a therapeutic alliance. Yet the patient's behaviors threaten to create a misalliance. You encourage engagement, but the patient has learned to disengage from people who hurt him. We can get frustrated when we forget that these behaviors are just the patient's implicit knowledge of how relationships work.

If we notice our frustration, we can use that as a signal: "Oh, an avoidance strategy is frustrating me." But if we take the frustration as personal—a patient frustrating us—we might make one of several common mistakes. We might implicitly criticize the patient. We might become pushy, trying to push the patient not to do what he has learned to do. We might challenge behaviors he does not see and does not knowingly use. However, it's important to remember that the patient does what he has learned was adaptive. He doesn't know what else to do. Whenever you encounter an avoidance strategy, point it out *and* always invite alliance behavior.

Principle: *When an avoidance strategy occurs, point it out, block it, and offer an alliance behavior.*

Here are two examples.

Example One

Pt: I don't know what my problem is. [*Insecure attachment behavior.*]

Th: Yet, if you had no problem, you wouldn't be here. [*Remind the patient of reality.*] So, what is the problem you would like us to help you with? [*Encourage a secure attachment.*]

Example Two

Pt: What do you think my problem is? [*Insecure attachment behavior.*]

Th: I don't know since I'm not you. [*Remind the patient of reality.*] That's why I have to ask you what problem you would like us to work on. [*Encourage a secure attachment.*]

When frustrated, we may mistakenly challenge patients' behavior, but avoidance behavior is usually the best relational knowledge they have. This is how they were taught to relate. The patient does not consciously frustrate you. Instead, he is unconsciously revealing the history of his frustration: the insecure attachment. Do not act on your frustration; use it as a signal to intervene. Identify the patient's avoidance strategy, block it, and then offer a secure attachment by inviting him to share his problem.

Skill-Building Exercise Six: Helping When Patients Ask What They Should Work On

Sometimes, patients ask, "What should I work on?" But since you aren't the patient, you can't know what they should work on.

Th: What is the problem you would like me to help you with?

Pt: What do you think I should focus on?

Th: Only you can know what you should focus on. [*Remind the patient of reality.*] So, what is the problem you would like me to help you with?

Again, notice how the patient operates according to the rules of an insecure attachment. "I know I shouldn't offer a problem, so tell me how to fit in with your insecure attachment." You cannot comment on her relational behavior. Why? She has not Yet, offered a problem to work on. That's why we block her avoidance strategy and return the focus to the problem she wants help with.

Watch a demonstration of how to help a patient recognize what she wants to work on at HTRBook .com/Video-16.

Practice a role-play exercise on working with a patient who asks you to tell him what his problem is at HTRBook.com/Audio-12.

As the patient in this role-play exercise, read the following to your partner who is in the therapist role. "I will play a patient who keeps asking you, the therapist, what you want me to work on. Block that avoidance strategy by reminding me of reality, then return to the focus on a problem. Begin this role-play of a session by asking me, 'What is the problem you would like me to help you with?'"

Pt: Where should I start? [*"I don't know because I don't know the problem you would like me to help you with. So, what is the problem you would like me to help you with?"*]

Pt: What should I talk about? [*"I don't know. Only you could know what problem you should talk about. What is the problem you would like me to help you overcome?"*]

Pt: Do you think I belong here? [*"I don't know. That's what we are here to find out. What is the problem you want me to help you with?"*]

Pt: Do you think drinking is a problem? [*"Only you can know if drinking is a problem for you. That's why I have to ask what the problem is you would like me to help you with."*]

Pt: Do you think I need therapy? [*"That's what we are here to find out. So, to figure that out, what is the problem you would like me to help you with?"*]

Pt: I was hoping you could tell me what to work on. [*"I have no right to tell you what to work on. Only you have the right to make that decision for yourself. So, what is the problem you would like me to help you with?" We have no right to tell the patient what to do. Only the patient has the right to make that decision. If you tell patients what to do, they will comply with you or defy you. Either response results in a misalliance.*]

Pt: You probably think I have a drug problem. [*"Only you can know if you have a drug problem. So, what is the problem you would like me to help you with?"*]

Pt: Do you think I have a problem? [*"Only you can know if you have a problem. So, what is the problem you would like me to help you with?"*]

Pt: Do you think I should be more intimate with my husband? [*"Only you can know if you should be more intimate with him. So, what is the problem you would like me to help you with?"*]

Pt: I know you therapists seem to think patients should share stuff with you. But I don't see why I should. [*"Only you can know if you should share with me. Obviously, if you don't want to, you don't have to. It's just that whatever you conceal, I can't help you with. So, what is the problem you would like me to help you with?"*]

Pt: So, what are we supposed to do here, doctor? [*"You aren't supposed to do anything. The question is what you want to do. If you have a problem you would like me to help you with, we can help you with that problem. If you don't have a problem to work on, there would be nothing to do. So, what is the problem you would like me to help you with?"*]

Pt: What are you wanting from me? [*"Nothing. The question is what you want from therapy. What is the problem you would like me to help you with?"*]

Pt: You probably think I have a problem. [*"I can't know that because I am not you. Only you can know whether you have a problem you would like me to help you with."*]

Pt: I suppose you think I should talk about my drug use. [*"Only you can know whether talking about your drug use would be good for you. So, what is the problem you would like me to help you with?"*]

Pt: You will say I should have sex with my husband, but I don't want to. [*"Only you can know whether you should have sex with your husband. So, what is the problem you would like me to help you with?"*]

Pt: What do you think I should talk about here? [*"Only you can know what you should talk about that would be good for you. What is the problem you would like me to help you with?"*]

Pt: I should probably talk about my relationship with my husband. He's threatening to divorce me. [*"And is this a problem for you that you want to work on for your benefit?"*]

Pt: [*Sighs.*] Yes.

Therapy must address the problem the patient thinks she should work on, not the problem you think she should work on. As long as you block the avoidance strategy and return the focus to the problem, your answer will be fine. The goal here is not to repeat the words in the book but to learn the principle guiding those words: remind the patient of reality and return to the problem.

Now let's continue the role-play exercise. The person in the patient role should read the following to the person in the therapist role. "Now we'll repeat the exercise. As soon as you, the therapist, intervene, I, the patient, will go immediately to the next patient statement. Let's make this exercise feel like a real session. We won't stop to chat during the exercise. Instead, we'll go straight through so you, the therapist, get the experience of processing and intervening more quickly. We'll repeat this until you have mastered it. Then we'll change roles and do it again until I have mastered it too."

Questions to ask each other to strengthen your skills: What did you learn about this strategy when the patient asked you what to work on? How does this change your previous understanding of this strategy? What did you learn when you didn't answer her question and instead let her answer it for herself? What did you feel when you kept the focus on what the patient thinks is her problem? In the patient role, what did you feel when the therapist ensured that you would be the one to say what to work on? What did you learn in the patient role that you hadn't realized before? What kind of relationship did the patient invite you to have when she asked, "What do you think I should work on?" Did your therapist speak to you in a kind, realistic tone of voice or with a hint of criticism or impatience? What advice do you have for your partner to speak in a kind, realistic tone of voice? How will this skill change your way of working?

Skill-Building Exercise Seven: Review Exercise

To maintain an effective focus in therapy, block avoidance strategies and return to the therapeutic focus. Without this skill, sessions remain chaotic, guided by the patient's avoidance strategies, and then the patient cannot declare her problem in therapy and get the help she needs.

For a review exercise of the skills you've been practicing, go to HTRBook.com/Audio-13.

As the patient in this role-play exercise, read the following to your partner who is in the therapist role. "Now you will learn to address many different strategies flexibly so you can integrate everything you have learned so far. In this role-play exercise, I'll play a patient who offers you either an internal problem or an avoidance strategy. When I use an avoidance strategy, block it and restate the question. You can start now and ask, 'What is the problem you would like me to help you with?'"

Pt: Well, the people at human resources said I have to get clean, or I won't have a job. [*"That's their opinion. But what is your opinion? What is the problem you want me to help you with?" Block the attribution of a problem to other people.*]

Pt: The people at intake said I have to come to see a therapist. [*"Since they aren't here, I can't help them. So, what is the internal problem you would like me to help you with?" Block his attribution onto the intake staff.*]

Pt: My wife said I should come. [*"But you came instead." Point out the contradiction between what he says (denial) and what he does (comes to your office).*]

Pt: My wife says I have a problem with depression. [*"That is her opinion. What is yours?" Blocking.*]

Pt: You should ask my wife. She's the one who thinks I ought to be here. [*"Since she is not here, I can't ask her. So, what is the problem you would like me to help you with?" Block the attribution to his wife.*]

Pt: I think my wife is the problem. [*"You say your wife is the problem, but you came instead." Point out the contradiction between what he says (attributes the problem to the wife) and what he does (comes to the session).*]

Pt: My wife is always nagging me. [*"How is that an internal problem for you?" Block the attribution to his wife.*]

Pt: My wife should be here. [*"And Yet, you came instead." Point out the contradiction between what he says and does.*]

Pt: There are real problems in our marriage. I think my wife is mentally ill, and I am hoping you could tell me how to talk to her and deal with her. [*"Since I don't know her, that's not something I can do. So, what is the internal problem you would like me to help you with?" Block the attribution to his wife.*]

Pt: Did anyone ever tell you? You have beautiful eyes. [*"Thank you. Coming back to your problem, what is the problem you would like me to help you with?" Block the avoidance strategy and return to the focus.*]

Pt: This is a nice office. Did you decorate it yourself? I like your choice of colors. [*"Thanks. Coming back to your problem, what is the problem that you would like me to help you with?" Block the avoidance strategy and return to the focus.*]

Pt: Do you think I have a problem? [*"Only you can know for sure if you have a problem, so what is the problem you would like my help with." Block the attribution to you.*]

Pt: But what do you think I should focus on, doctor? [*"I have no idea. That's why I have to ask you what the problem is you would like me to help you with."*]

Pt: I was hoping you could tell me what my problem is. [*"Only you can know for sure what the problem is you want to work on. So, what is the problem you would like me to help you with?"*]

Pt: I am suffering from diabetes after drinking for so many years. [*"That is a medical problem that I can't help you with. So, what is the psychological problem you would like my help with?" Differentiate a nonpsychological from a psychological problem.*]

Pt: I have a drinking problem. [*"How is that an internal emotional problem for you?"*]

Pt: My wife has a real problem with men. She can't stand assertive men, so she constantly puts me down. I think she should get some therapy. [*"You have described your wife, but it's still not clear what the internal problem is you would like me to help you with. What is the problem you would like me to help you with?" Block the strategy of blaming others (I don't cause my suffering; my wife does.)*]

Pt: First, I should probably tell you that I first started using drugs at age thirteen. You are the fifteenth shrink I have seen in the past forty years. [*"Before we go into your history, what is the problem is you would like me to help you with?" Block the use of history to avoid revealing an internal problem.*]

Pt: I've been depressed ever since I lost my job. [*"And would you like me to help you overcome this depression?" Since the patient declared a problem, we can ask if it is his will to work on it together.*]

Pt: [*Sighs*] Yes. [*"Could we look at when your depression started?"*]

That was challenging, wasn't it? In real life, a patient doesn't use just one avoidance strategy. Thus, we need many skills to help the patient form a working alliance. As long as you block the avoidance strategy and return the focus to the problem, your answer will be fine. The goal here is not to repeat the words in the book but to learn the principle guiding those words.

Now let's continue the role-play exercise. The person in the patient role should read the following to the person in the therapist role. "Now we'll repeat the exercise. As soon as you, the therapist, intervene, I, the patient, will go immediately to the next patient statement. Let's make this exercise feel like a real session. We won't stop to chat during the exercise. Instead, we'll go straight through so you, the therapist, get the experience of processing and intervening more quickly. We'll repeat this until you have mastered it. Then we'll change roles and do it again until I have mastered it too."

Questions to ask each other to strengthen your skills: What did you learn from using different skills to avoid declaring a problem? What do you understand now about avoiding declaring a problem that you did not understand before? What did you feel as you maintained a consistent therapeutic focus in the face of so many avoidance strategies? In the patient role, what did you feel as the therapist maintained a consistent therapeutic focus? What did you learn about the patient's experience of a consistent therapeutic focus? How will this change your work with patients who use avoidance strategies? How is this experience of maintaining a therapeutic focus changing your understanding of the therapist's role?

For a summary of the skills you've been learning, go to HTRBook.com/Video-17.

Skill-Building Exercise Eight: Handling Denial of a Problem

Sometimes the patient comes into therapy and says, "I have no problem." In response, the therapist is often stunned. What do I do now? Why is she here? A patient comes to therapy and denies she has a problem requiring therapy? That seems crazy!

How might it be perfectly sensible? In an insecure attachment, a child might deny that she has a problem to please a parent who doesn't want one. Perhaps you have heard the term "problem child." In an insecure attachment, a caretaker may label a child with a typical problem as a problem child. Thus, the child will deny she has a problem so her parent can love her again until the next time she needs help.

When a patient denies that she has a problem, sometimes she invites you to tell her that she does. This would create a will battle between you, who believes she has a problem, and the patient, who believes she doesn't. Instead, we need to help the patient see how her denial conflicts with reality, not with you.

Sometimes we make the mistake of trying to convince the patient that she has a problem. For example, "But didn't you say you are recovering from alcoholism?" Then the patient argues with you, denying that she has a problem by saying she is in AA or claiming that it occurred in the past.

Another mistake we make is "fishing." "Do you have problems in your marriage?" "How is your work life?" In response to our fishing, the patient gives nothing. There are no problems with her wife. Her work life is fine. Finally, exasperated, we may blurt out, "So, why are you here?" In response to this premature confrontation, the patient will reply, "Beats me. I told you I don't have a problem."

So, how do we deal with denial? We mirror it.

Th: What's the problem you would like me to help you with?

Pt: I don't have a problem.

Th: Wonderful. [*Mirroring denial.*]

The patient is prepared for an argument that she has won many times. Don't pick up the bait. Instead, mirror her denial. When she cannot have a conflict with you, she will be in conflict with her denial. Then, *her* problems will rise to the surface from within *her*.

Watch a demonstration of how to work with denial at HTRBook.com/Video-18.

Practice working with denial in the skill-building exercise at HTRBook.com/Audio-14.

As the patient in this role-play exercise, read the following to your partner who is in the therapist role. "When I say that I have no problem, mirror my denial: 'Wonderful. You are a lucky person.' Or, 'Good for you.' Continue mirroring my denial until I reveal my problem. Now we will begin the role-play exercise. I will offer different forms of denial. Then you will mirror my denial so the patient's denial conflicts with her wish for help, not with you. Go ahead and ask, 'What is the problem you would like me to help you with?'"

Pt: I have no topic to talk about today. [*"Someone who has no topic to talk about comes to a therapist's office. Yet, I'm sure you would not come for no reason."*]

Pt: I don't have a problem. [*"Wonderful."*]

Pt: Everything is going great. [*"That's great. If only everyone were so lucky."*]

Pt: No problem I can think of. I used to have a problem, but it's resolved now. [*"So, you used to have a problem, but now it's resolved. That's great."*]

Pt: Yeah, it is. I can't think of anything right now that is giving me any trouble. [*"Nothing is giving you trouble right now. Good." When any cues of health emerge, repeat those words to establish a relationship with her wish to get well.*]

Pt: Things are going well. The marriage is going well. [*"Things are going well. The marriage is going well."*]

Pt: Yeah. Really well. [*"Really well. Fantastic." "Really" is a sign of heavier denial, thus, feelings are rising. Mirror his heavier denial.*]

Pt: [*Sighs.*] Well, I don't know about fantastic. But, yeah, really well. [*"So, maybe not fantastic, but really well. That's wonderful." Mirror her healthier response: "not fantastic."*]

Pt: Uh. Yeah. I mean, coming here was just to satisfy my wife, you know. She thought I should see someone, so I figured, what the heck. If it makes her happy, why not? [*"She thought you should see someone. You didn't think you needed to see someone. But you came here, figuring, what the heck, I'll satisfy my wife."*]

Pt: [*Sighs.*] Uh. Yeah. Well, uh, I don't like the sound of that. [*"Even though you don't like the sound of it, you did it anyway."*]

Pt: [*Sighs.*] Well, like I said, I don't think I have a problem. [*"That's great. A lot of people would like to be in your position." Progress: first, she said she had no problem. Now she says that she does* not *think* she has a problem.*]

Pt: [*Sighs.*] Well, uh, I mean, I don't mean to say there are no problems in my life. [*"You don't mean to say there are no problems in your life, maybe just no problems that require therapy." Progress: not no problems = I have problems. Her admission emerges through a double negative.*]

Pt: [*Sighs.*] Exactly. [*"Fantastic."*]

Pt: [*Sighs.*] I mean, a lot of people are like that, aren't they? [*"Absolutely. A lot of people have problems that don't require therapy. And it may be that your problems don't need the help of a therapist."*]

Pt: Except that she said she's thinking about getting a divorce. [*"Just because she wants a divorce though doesn't mean you have to deal with your problems in therapy." Mirror denial of a problem until he declares one.*]

Pt: [*Sighs.*] But I don't want to lose her. [*"So, what do you want us to do here?"*]

Pt: I guess I should talk about what's going on with the two of us. [*"But do you want to? After all, I have no right to ask you to talk about this unless this is what you want for yourself?" His use of*

"I guess" and *"should"* show that he is still hesitant. That's why we still need to address his lack of
will. Don't move forward until he wants to.]

Pt: [*Sighs.*] I guess I'm hesitating here like I do with her. [*"And that's okay. If you are hesitant, I
have no right to explore anything about your marriage unless that is what you want to do for
yourself."*]

Pt: [*Sighs.*] If I don't, I'll lose her. [*"Not wanting to lose her and at the same time tempted to hesitate
even if it means you lose her." Mirror his conflict without taking sides. That way, the conflict
remains in him, not between the two of you.*]

Pt: [*Sighs.*] I can't lose her. [*"That's not true. If you hesitate longer, you can lose her." Remind her of
reality.*]

Pt: [*Sobs.*]

That was hard, wasn't it! Sometimes therapists are tempted to argue with the patient's denial.
Instead, let the patient experience how her denial conflicts with her desires, not with you. As long
as you mirror the denial, your answer will be fine. The goal here is not to repeat the words in the
book but to learn the principle guiding those words.

Now let's continue the role-play exercise. The person in the patient role should read the following to the person in the therapist role. "Now we'll repeat the exercise. As soon as you, the
therapist, intervene, I, the patient, will go immediately to the next patient statement. Let's make
this exercise feel like a real session. We won't stop to chat. Instead, we'll go straight through so you,
the therapist, get the experience of processing and intervening more quickly. We'll repeat this until
you have mastered it. Then we'll change roles and do it again until I have mastered it too."

Questions to ask each other to strengthen your skills: What did you feel as you continually blocked
denial? What did you learn by letting go of any agenda? In the patient role, what did you feel when
your therapist avoided being in conflict with your denial? What did you learn in the patient role?
How does that change your understanding of how to work with denial? What did you learn as you
let the patient have her conflict without your getting into conflict with her denial? How does this
change your understanding of the therapeutic alliance? Did your partner sound sarcastic, or did
your partner empathically accept your struggle? How might you advise your partner to accept the
patient as she is?

CHAPTER FIVE

Is It Safe to Have a Separate Mind and Will in Therapy?

Some patients become very anxious when they depend on a therapist, a sign that depending was dangerous in the past. Other patients automatically hide their problems, thereby revealing how they dealt with that danger. And other patients may reveal a problem but not declare their will to work on it. These patients often grew up in homes where it was dangerous to have a separate mind or will. So, they show us how they dealt with that danger: they learned to comply with the will of others by hiding their separate mind and will. Thus, we have to help them feel safe enough to declare their own will so that their will drives their therapy. Then the therapist can be the servant of the patient's will to health.

Principle for Declaring One's Will:

When patients attribute their will to others, help them own their will so therapy will be driven by their will and no one else's.

STAGE THREE: DECLARING ONE'S WILL TO WORK ON THE PROBLEM

To develop a therapeutic alliance, we need to know the problem the patient seeks our help for. Then we find out whether she wants to work on her problem. Having a problem is not enough; the patient must *want* to work on it (Davanloo 2002–2004; Miller and Rollnick, 2012; Rank 1936). If the therapist wants to work on the problem, but the patient doesn't, therapy can't go anywhere. Therapy works only if the patient works.

However, patients often learned not to say what they wanted. An abuser ignores and dismisses the child's will. He asks the child to want what she doesn't want. Children learn that declaring a separate will is dangerous. As a result, in therapy, patients may avoid declaring their will to work on a problem. Then we won't have a working alliance. The following exercises will focus on how to help patients who avoid declaring their will to work on a problem.

You do not ask questions to get the answer you want. Instead, you invite a working alliance that is driven by what the patient wants. The patient may avoid declaring her will for a while as part of an unconscious test of you: "Is it safe for me to declare my will in this relationship with the therapist?" When you understand the patient's relational plight, you can persistently invite the patient to declare her will to work on her problem. By doing so, you demonstrate that you will follow her will, and her desires will drive the therapy.

Skill-Building Exercise One: Inviting the Experience of Will

Many patients were hurt in earlier relationships if they said what they wanted. As a result, they hesitate to declare their will to work on their problem. Or they declare their will but with no enthusiasm or determination.

We should not assume that the patient wants to work on a problem when she declares one. Instead, we should check. We have no right to explore if she does not want to. So, we ask whether she wants to work on her problem. She can respond in one of three ways:

1. *Will*: She says she wants to work on her problem with real determination and sighs, indicating a rise of anxiety in the somatic nervous system due to her choice to face what she usually avoids.
2. *Anxiety*: She may become overwhelmed with anxiety.
3. *Avoidance strategy*: She may say she does not want to (defiance). Or she may say she wants to but without real determination (compliance). She defies or complies with what she thinks you want.

If she responds with high anxiety, help her see how her wish to do something good for herself makes her anxious. If she responds with an avoidance strategy, block her strategy and keep asking whether she wants to work on her problem. If she avoids what makes her anxious, no anxiety will rise. So, we will not see a sigh. However, if she decides to face what she usually avoids, anxiety will rise. Then we will see a sigh. Once she sighs, her will is online, and we can go to the next step: exploring a specific example.

See how to invite the patient to declare her will to do therapy at HTRBook.com/Video-19.
Practice helping the patient declare her will to do therapy at HTRBook.com/Audio-15.

As the patient in this role-play exercise, read the following to your partner who is in the therapist role. "In this exercise, ask whether I want to work on my problem. In response, I will respond with avoidance strategies. When I declare my will but do not sigh, ask how I experience my wish to work on my problem. When I say that other people want me to work on my problem, block this avoidance strategy and ask about my will.

"In this example, I have declared a problem, but I did not sound like I was motivated to work on it. Begin the role-play exercise by asking, 'Is this a problem you would like to work on here with me?'"

Pt: [*No sigh. Diffident voice.*] Sure. [*"What tells you inside that you know you want to do this for yourself?" The absence of a sigh, unconscious anxiety, means that will is not online. So, the therapy cannot move beyond this point until we see an unconscious cue that the patient's will is online.*]

Pt: If you think I should. [*"But do you want to for yourself?"*]

Pt: [*No sigh.*] Okay. [*"What tells you inside that you know you want to do this for yourself?"*]

Pt: I know I should. [*"But do you want to for yourself?"*]

Pt: Mmm. [*"What tells you inside that you know you want to do this for yourself?"*]

Pt: I'm here. I know that's what we're supposed to do. [*"But what tells you inside that you know you want to do this for yourself?"*]

Pt: [*Flat voice, no sigh.*] I want to work on my problems. [*"Are you sure?"*]

Pt: [*Said in a detached voice.*] Yeah. [*"What tells you inside that you know you want to do this for you?"*]

Pt: If you think it's a good idea. [*"The question is whether you think it's a good idea for you. Do you want to work on this problem for yourself?"*]

Pt: I have to. [*"That's not true. You don't* have *to work on any problem. The question is whether you* want *to work on your problem for your benefit."*]

Pt: My wife thinks I should. [*"But this can't be her therapy. That's why we have to find out whether you want to work on this problem. If you don't want to, I have no right to ask you to do something you don't want to do."*]

Pt: What do you think? [*"I don't know because I'm not you. That's why I have to ask whether you want to work on your problem for your benefit."*]

Pt: Maybe I don't want to. [*"Okay. If you don't want to, I have to respect your wish. It just means we won't be able to help you with your problem."*]

Pt: So, what am I supposed to do? [*"You aren't* supposed *to do anything here. The question, is what do you* want *to do?"*]

Pt: I feel like you are wanting something from me. [*"I don't need anything from you because this isn't my problem. The question is whether you want to work on your problem for your benefit. If you don't want to work on your problem, I have to respect your wish."*]

Pt: But how will I get anywhere then? [*"Good that you are asking yourself that question. You're asking the right person."*]

Pt: [*Sighs.*] I don't feel totally committed to this. [*"What level of noncommitment to your goal do you think would be optimal for you?"*]

Pt: [*Sighs.*] When you put it that way, it sounds ridiculous. [*"Just because it sounds ridiculous doesn't mean you should commit to your goal. You have every right not to commit to your goal."*]

Pt: [*Sighs.*] I know. I know. Okay. I have to work on this. Otherwise, I'm going to remain stuck. [*"You don't have to. The question is, do you want to work on this problem for your benefit?"*]

Pt: [*Sighs.*] Yes. [*"What's a specific example of your problem you would like us to look at?"*]

The therapist never explored a specific example until the patient stopped attributing her will to the therapist, said she wanted to work on her problem, and sighed when she said so. The sigh is critical. Without a sigh, we have compliance. The lips say yes, but the body says no (lack of sighing, emotion, or energy in the body).

Three main obstacles prevent us from developing an effective alliance with patients: (1) unregulated anxiety, (2) no declared problem to work on, and (3) no will to explore that problem. If you move forward without the patient's will, therapy remains stuck. The patient will comply with what she thinks you want, or she will defy what she thinks you want. Don't move forward until she declares her will and sighs when she does so. As long as you block the avoidance strategy and return the focus to the patient's will, your answer will be fine. The goal here is not to repeat the words in the book but to learn the principle guiding those words: the patient's will is the engine of therapy.

Now let's continue the role-play exercise. The person in the patient role should read the following to the person in the therapist role. "Now we'll repeat the exercise. As soon as you, the therapist, intervene, I, the patient, will go immediately to the next patient statement. Let's make this exercise feel like a real session. We won't stop for talking. We'll go straight through so you, the therapist, get the experience of processing and intervening more quickly. We'll repeat this until you have mastered it. Then we'll change roles and do it again until I have mastered it too."

Questions to ask each other to strengthen your skills: What did you learn about mobilizing the patient's will? How does this change your previous understanding of patient motivation? What did you feel as you let go of your agenda and asked for the patient's will? What did you feel as you let the patient's will drive the therapy? In the patient role, what did you feel when the therapist kept focusing on your will and desire? What did you learn when the therapist kept that focus? How does this change your understanding of where the motivation lies in therapy? What do you understand about the patient's will in therapy that you did not understand before? What are you learning about being the servant of the patient's will? Was your partner in the therapist role able to accept the patient's right not to explore, or was your partner's voice critical? How could your partner convey more acceptance of the patient's right to say no?

Skill-Building Exercise Two: Attributing the Will to Do Therapy on to Others

When we ask if the patient wants to work on his problem, he may say that someone else wants him to. That makes sense from the perspective of an insecure attachment. "I know the rules. I must hide my will to keep this relationship. I must follow your will instead." This understanding will allow you to block the patient's avoidance strategy while inviting a therapeutic alliance. Without his will, we have no right to do therapy.

Practice ways to get the patient's will online at HTRBook.com/Audio-16.

As the patient in this role-play exercise, read the following to your partner who is in the therapist role. "You, in the therapist role, will ask if I would like to take a look at this problem. I will say that someone else wants me to. Block my attribution of will onto others by asking whether it is my will to work on my problem. Begin the role-play exercise by asking, 'Would you like to take a look at this problem?'"

Pt: My doctor said I should. [*"But is it your will to work on this problem for your benefit?"*]

Pt: My boss told me I have to come here. [*"But is it your will to work on this problem for your benefit?"*]

Pt: I know what my wife would say. [*"But is it your will to work on this problem for your benefit?"*]

Pt: My sponsor said I need to. [*"But is it your will to work on this problem for your benefit?"*]

Pt: My company said I have to be here. [*"I realize you may have to be here for the sake of your company, but I don't have to be here for the sake of your company. That's why I have to ask you whether this is a problem you want to work on for your benefit."*]

Pt: My wife says I have to get off drugs. [*"That's what your wife wants, but what do you want for yourself?"*]

Pt: I have to if I want to keep my job. [*"But do you want to work on this problem to achieve your goal?"*]

Pt: I don't know. [*"That's okay. I have no right to help you with this problem unless it is a problem you want to work on for your benefit. That's why I have to ask you: is this a problem you want to work on for your benefit?"*]

Pt: Ask my foreman. He's the one who said I have to be in rehab. [*"It may have been his decision, but it can't be his rehab. That's why I have to ask you, do you want to work on this problem to achieve your goal?"*]

Pt: If I don't do this, my workplace will fire me. [*"But just because they would fire you doesn't mean you have to work on this problem. You have the right not to work on this problem. That's why I have to ask you: do you want to work on this problem for your benefit?"*]

Pt: My wife said I have to come to the clinic. [*"But just because you come to the clinic doesn't mean you have to resolve your problems. That's why I have to ask you: do you want to work on this problem for your benefit?"*]

Pt: What should we talk about? [*"The question is not what we should talk about but whether it is your will to work on your problem. Do you want to work on this problem for your benefit?"*]

Pt: What should I do here? [*"The question is not what you should do, but what you want to do. Do you want to work on your problem here for your benefit?"*]

Pt: I could tell you about my drug use if you think that would help. [*"I have no right to talk about your drug use unless you want to. So, do you want to talk about your drug use to get the help you want for your benefit?"*]

Pt: Well, since I'm here, I guess I'm supposed to look at my drug issues. [*"You are not supposed to do anything here. The question is, do you want to look at your drug issues to get the help you want for your benefit?"*]

Pt: [*Sighs.*] Yes. If I don't, I'll keep messing up. [*"So, can we look at a specific example where this problem comes up for you?" Before we explore a specific example, the patient must declare his will and sigh: the unconscious sign that his will is finally online.*]

That was hard, wasn't it? Since the patient's will is the engine of therapy, keep inviting his will until it is online. As long as you block the avoidance strategy and return the focus to the patient's will, your answer will be fine. The goal here is not to repeat the words in the book but to learn the principle guiding those words: the patient's will is the engine of therapy.

Now let's continue the role-play exercise. The person in the patient role should read the following to the person in the therapist role. "Let's do the exercise again. As soon as you, the therapist, intervene, I, the patient, will go to the next patient statement. To make this exercise feel like a real session, we won't stop to chat. Let's go straight through so you, the therapist, get the experience of processing and intervening more quickly. We'll repeat this exercise until you master it. Then we'll change roles and do it again until I master it too."

Questions to ask each other to strengthen your skills: What did you feel when you kept the focus on the patient's will and blocked his attributions to others? What shifted within you as you let go of your desire and focused on his instead? In the patient role, what did you feel when your therapist constantly focused on what you wanted? What did you feel when you could not get the therapist to try to control you? As the therapist, what did you learn about letting go of trying to control the patient? What are you learning about being the servant of the patient's will? How does being the servant of the patient's will change your understanding of your role as a therapist?

Skill-Building Exercise Three: Attributing the Will to Do Therapy on to the Therapist

Sometimes your patient will attribute his will to do therapy to you. In those cases, you will have to block that avoidance strategy.

Practice a skill-building exercise on working with a patient who attributes the will to do therapy to you at HTRBook.com/Audio-17.

As the patient in this role-play exercise, read the following to your partner who is in the therapist role. "When you ask whether the patient wants to work on his problem, he may attribute his will to you. But therapy cannot be based on your will, only on his. Block the patient's avoidance strategy and see if he can own his will to do therapy to achieve his goals. Unless he wants to work on his problem, we have no right to do therapy with him. Go ahead and ask, 'Would you like to take a look at this problem?'"

Pt: Do you think I should work on this drinking issue? [*"Only you can know for sure whether drinking is a problem for you. You have the right not to work on your drinking if it's not a problem for you."*]

Pt: Do you think I need rehab? [*"Only you can know whether you need rehab. This problem may not be something you want to work on in rehab."*]

Pt: I was hoping you could tell me. [*"I have no right to tell you that you need rehab. Only you have the right to make that decision for yourself. That's why I have to ask you whether this is a problem you want to work on for your benefit."*]

Pt: You probably think I should work on this. [*"Only you can know if you should work on this problem. If you don't want to work on this problem, I have no right to help you resolve something you don't want to resolve."*]

Pt: Do you want to look at it? [*"I don't need to look at it since it's not my problem. That's why I have to ask you. Since it is your problem, do you want to work on it for your benefit?"*]

Pt: Do you agree with my boss that I should? I haven't worked on it before. [*"Only you can know whether you should work on your problem. If you haven't worked on it before, there is no law that says you have to work on it now."*]

Pt: I'm hoping you can pull something out of me. [*"Only you can pull something out of yourself. I can't do that. So, the question is, do you want to pull something out of yourself so that you get better information and can make better decisions for yourself?"*]

Pt: I know you therapists seem to think patients should share stuff with you. But I don't see why I should. [*"Only you can know whether you should share with me. Obviously, if you don't want to, you don't have to. It's just that whatever you conceal, we can't heal. So, is it your will to work on this problem for your benefit?"*]

Pt: Okay. So, what am I supposed to do? [*"You don't have to do anything. If you want to work on a problem for your benefit, we can work on it. If you don't want to work on a problem, I have to respect your wish to stay the way you are. If what you are doing is working for you, you should keep doing what works."*]

Pt: What are you wanting from me? [*"Nothing. The question is, what do you want from therapy? Is it your wish to work on this problem for your benefit?"*]

Pt: I suppose you think I should. [*"Only you can know for sure whether you should do this for your benefit. I have no right to tell you what to want for yourself."*]

Pt: Do you think I should talk about my problems? [*"Only you can know whether talking about your problems would be good for you. Do you want to talk about your problems to achieve your goals?"*]

Pt: This is different. I'm used to therapies where people tell me what do. [*"But then you would be following what they want rather than doing what you want. That's why we need to find out whether this is a problem that you want to work on for your benefit."*]

Pt: Maybe. This is certainly different.

Do not try to be the engine of the therapy. Since the patient's will is the engine of therapy, keep inviting his will until it is online. As long as you block the patient's attribution of his will to you and return the focus to his will, your answer will be fine. The goal here is not to repeat the words in the book but to learn the principle guiding those words: the patient's will is the engine of therapy.

Now let's continue the role-play exercise. The person in the patient role should read the following to the person in the therapist role. "Now we'll repeat the exercise. As soon as you, the therapist, intervene, I, the patient, will go immediately to the next patient statement. Let's make this exercise feel like a real session. We won't stop for talking. We'll go straight through so you, the therapist, get the experience of processing and intervening more quickly. We'll repeat this until you have mastered it. Then we'll change roles and do it again until I have mastered it too."

Questions to ask each other to strengthen your skills: What did you feel as you held a therapeutic position without taking sides in the patient's conflict? What new understanding developed as you held onto this therapeutic position? In the patient role, what did you feel while your therapist constantly avoided taking sides in your conflict? What did you feel when you could not get the therapist to be the engine of therapy? How is this experience changing your understanding of how patients can attribute their will to other people? As the therapist, what are you learning as you let go of being the engine of the therapy?

Skill-Building Exercise Four: Deactivating Patients' Defiance

Sometimes patients do not declare what they want. Instead, they imagine that other people want something out of them. Then they defy the will they attribute to others. First, they claim they don't want to do therapy. Next, they assume *you* want them to do therapy. Then they defy you and argue with you.

Do not argue with the patient. That supports his defiance. Instead, remind him of reality to block the attribution of will. Here's an example:

Th: Would you like to work on this problem?

Pt: No. I don't want to work on it.

Th: Okay. I have no right to ask you to work on something you don't want to work on.

It must be the patient's will to do therapy. Your will is not enough. If you give 100 percent of your will and the patient gives only 10 percent of his will, he will get a 10 percent result. Often, we try to give 190 percent to make up for the 90 percent the patient withholds. That never works. Why? You can give only your 100 percent. You can never give what the patient withholds *from himself.* Only he can give what he withholds. As long as a patient defies you, undo his defiance by reminding him of reality.

Practice your skills of dealing with defiance at HTRBook.com/Audio-18.

As the patient in this role-play exercise, read the following to your partner who is in the therapist role. "When the patient defies you, remind him of reality. His behavior is in conflict with the demands of reality, not with you. I will play a patient who defies you. Go ahead and ask, 'Would you like to work on this problem?'"

Pt: I'm not sure. [*"If you're not sure, I have no right to ask you to work on something you don't want to work on."*]

Pt: I'm afraid to face what's underneath. [*"You can face what you fear so you can be in charge. Or you can avoid what you fear, and then the fear will be in charge of you. But the choice is yours."*]

Pt: No. I don't want to look at it. [*"Okay."*]

Pt: I like feeling in control, and I don't like getting into something I don't understand. [*"If you don't want to get into something, I have no right to ask you to get into it."*]

Pt: I don't want to work on it. [*"Okay."*]

Pt: [*Waits five seconds before responding.*] You probably think I should work on this, but I don't want to. [*"Why work on this problem if you don't want to?" Notice how during the silence, your anxiety rose? When anxiety rises in you, it is often rising in the patient. If you can listen without talking, the patient will speak first, and you will get a better response from the patient.*]

Pt: What if I don't want to work on this? [*"Then I have to respect your wish. But then you would get no help for your problem."*]

Pt: So, can I go? [*"You can have as little help as you want. I have no right to ask you to work on a problem if you don't want to work on a problem for your benefit."*]

Pt: Are you kicking me out? [*"No. You said you don't want to work on your problem. So, you haven't entered therapy yet. And you can't be kicked out of a therapy you have not Yet, entered. And that's okay. This may not be the right time for you to do therapy."*]

Pt: Maybe it's not the right time. [*"It may not be the right time for you to work on your problems. Maybe a later time would be better."*]

Pt: I'd like to wait until later. [*"You have a right to wait as long as you want before you work on your problems. Why rush yourself?"*]

Pt: I sense you think I should stay and work on my issues. [*"Only you can know if staying and working on your issues would be in your interest."*]

Pt: I feel you are putting the ball back in my court. [*"But whose problem are we talking about?"*]

Pt: Mine. [*"Right. So, I can't put your problem back into you; it's been there all along. The only question is whether it's a problem for you that you want to work on now. And it may not be something you want to work on right now."*]

Pt: Right. I don't see it as a problem I need to work on. [*"Good that you are so clear. Why work on a problem you don't think you need to work on?"*]

Pt: So, are you saying I have to leave? [*"No. Since you said you don't want to work on your problem, you haven't entered therapy yet. You can't leave a therapy you haven't entered."*]

Pt: But I'm here. [*"But being here isn't enough. We would have to work together on your problem to achieve your goals. And if you don't want to do that right now, we have to respect your wish to wait."*]

Pt: So, are you saying I have to do therapy or I have to leave? [*"You have a right not to work on your problems. But if you don't want to work on your problems, this would just be a pretend therapy, and that would be a waste of your time and our effort."*]

Pt: What if I don't want to? [*"Why make yourself do therapy if you don't want to? Why do that to yourself?"*]

Pt: Aren't you supposed to try to convince me to do therapy? [*"I have no right to convince you to do something you don't want to do. Why look at your problem if that is not what you want for yourself?"*]

Pt: I thought that's what therapists did: convince patients. [*"No. If you are not convinced that you should look at your problems, I have no right to ask you to do something you don't want to do."*]

Pt: So, you're not going to make me work on my problem? [*"No. I can't make you work on anything. Only you can make yourself work on your problems. If you don't want to, I have to respect the facts: you may not want to right now."*]

Pt: So, what if we look at a problem later and not now? [*"Then we would have a nontherapy now while waiting for an imaginary therapy in the future. Why waste your time doing that?"*]

Pt: So, you are okay with me not working on a problem? [*"Absolutely. If you don't want to work on a problem, I have no right to ask you to do what you don't want to do."*]

Pt: But then I won't get better. [*"Oh."*]

Pt: Don't you care whether your patients get better? [*"Since you don't care whether your problems get resolved, apparently, you don't care whether you get better. I have to accept that you may not care about yourself just yet."*]

Pt: What if I don't care? [*"Then we would just have to accept that at this point in your life you don't care enough about yourself to work on your problems. And so we would not be able to do that together."*]

Pt: [*Waits five seconds before responding.*] Okay. I guess I have to work on this problem. [*"No. There's no law that says you have to work on your problem. The question is, do you* want *to work on your problem for your benefit? And, if you don't, that's okay. It may not be the time to get help."*]

Pt: No. If I don't get help now, I'll just keep making the same mistakes. [*"So, is it your will to work on your problem?"*]

Pt: [*Sighs.*] Yes. [*"What would be a specific example of your problem you would like us to take a look at?" Notice that we didn't explore a specific example until he declared his will, and he sighed.*]

Notice how long you may need to persist until the patient feels safe enough to declare his will to work with you. Since the patient's will is the engine of therapy, keep inviting his will until it is online. As long as you remind the patient that his strategy is in conflict with reality, not with you, your answer will be fine. The goal here is not to repeat the words in the book but to learn the principle guiding those words: the patient's will is the engine of therapy.

Now let's continue the role-play exercise. The person in the patient role should read the following to the person in the therapist role. "Now we'll repeat the exercise. As soon as you, the therapist, intervene, I, the patient, will go immediately to the next patient statement. Let's make this exercise feel like a real session. We won't stop for talking. We'll go straight through so you, the therapist, get the experience of processing and intervening more quickly. We'll repeat this until you have mastered it. Then we'll change roles and do it again until I have mastered it too."

Questions to ask each other to strengthen your skills: What did you feel when you held a therapeutic position without taking sides in the patient's conflict? In the patient role, what did you feel when your therapist avoided taking sides in your conflict? What did you feel when you could not get the therapist to be the engine of therapy? What do you understand now about the importance of the patient's will and desire that you didn't understand before doing this exercise? What you resist will persist. What did you learn about accepting the patient's defiance instead of defying it?

Skill-Building Exercise Five: Helping Patients with Anxiety When They Declare Their Will to Do Therapy

When patients say they want to work on a problem, they often become anxious. Why? They have decided to form a relationship where they work with you to do something good. Yet, their experience is that relationships lead to bad experiences rather than good ones.

Although the patient's new commitment to working together triggers her anxiety, she rarely realizes this. Help her identify and pay attention to her anxiety right away so she can bear the wish to do something good for herself.

Practice a skill-building exercise on helping patients heal with the anxiety that arises when they declare their will to do therapy at HTRBook.com/Audio-19.

As the patient in this role-play exercise, read the following to your partner who is in the therapist role. "In the following role-play, you will ask if it is my will to work on my problem. In response, I will describe a sign of anxiety. Then, identify my anxiety and point out how declaring my will triggers my anxiety. For instance, 'That's a sign of anxiety. Notice how saying that it is your will to look at your problem triggers this anxiety? Isn't that interesting?' We'll begin a series of role-plays. For the first one, ask, 'Is it your will to work on this problem?'"

Example One

Th: Is it your will to work on this problem?

Pt: [*Squirms in the chair.*] Yes. [*"What do you notice feeling when you say that?"*]

Pt: Anxious. [*"Notice how saying that you want to work on your problem makes you anxious?"*]

Pt: Yes. [*"Notice how this anxiety attacks you as if it is against the law to do something good for yourself?"*]

Example Two

Th: Is it your will to work on this problem?

Pt: [*Looks anxious.*] I think so. [*"What do you notice feeling when you say that?"*]

Pt: Nervous. [*"Notice how saying that you want to work on your problem makes you anxious?"*]

Pt: Yes. [*"Notice how this anxiety attacks you as if it is against the law to do something good for yourself?"*]

Example Three

Th: Is it your will to work on this problem?

Pt: [*Says nervously.*] Yes. [*"What do you notice feeling when you say that?"*]

Pt: Scared. [*"Notice how saying that you want to work on your problem makes you scared?"*]

Pt: Yes. [*"Notice how this anxiety attacks you as if it is against the law to do something good for yourself?"*]

Example Four

Th: Is it your will to work on this problem?

Pt: [*Says with a hesitant voice.*] Yeah. [*"What do you notice feeling when you say that?"*]

Pt: Uncomfortable. [*"Notice how saying that you want to work on your problem makes you uncomfortable?"*]

Pt: Yes. [*"Notice how this anxiety attacks you as if it is against the law to do something good for yourself?"*]

Example Five

Th: Is it your will to work on this problem?

Pt: Uh. Mmm. Well. Okay. [*"What do you notice feeling when you say that?"*]

Pt: I feel like I want to leave. [*"Notice how saying that you want help makes you want to leave the help you want?"*]

Pt: Yes. [*"Notice how this anxiety attacks you as if it is against the law to do something good for yourself?"*]

Help the patient see how wanting to do something good triggers anxiety. Now she realizes that revealing her desire feels risky. As long as you help the patient see how declaring her will makes her anxious, your answer will be fine. The goal here is not to repeat the words in the book but to learn the principle guiding those words: regulate anxiety caused by declaring one's will to do therapy.

Now let's continue the role-play exercise. The person in the patient role should read the following to the person in the therapist role. "Now we'll repeat the exercise. As soon as you, the therapist, intervene, I, the patient, will go immediately to the next patient statement. Let's make this exercise feel like a real session. We won't stop for talking. We'll go straight through so you, the therapist, get the experience of processing and intervening more quickly. We'll repeat this until you have mastered it. Then we'll change roles and do it again until I have mastered it too."

Questions to ask each other to strengthen your skills: What do you understand about the patient's will that you did not understand before? What did you learn in the patient role when the therapist addressed your anxiety about your will to do therapy? How does the patient's anxiety change your previous understanding of the danger of declaring her will to engage in therapy?

Skill-Building Exercise Six: Integrative Exercise: Moving from No Alliance to Alliance

We have covered a lot of skills and techniques so far. Before moving on to this integrative exercise, now would be a good time to practice all the skills you've learned so far.

For a review exercise, go to HTRBook.com/Audio-20.

This role-play exercise will help you move from no alliance to alliance. As the patient in this role-play exercise, read the following to your partner who is in the therapist role. "In this exercise, you will use every skill you have learned so far. You will begin therapy, and I will play a patient who presents with anxiety, avoidance strategies, or problems of will. Each time, intervene and return to your focus.

"Begin the role-play exercise. Ask, 'What is the problem you would like me to help you with?'"

Pt: I feel anxious. [*"Where do you notice feeling anxiety in your body?"*]

Pt: I am getting sick to my stomach. [*"This is a sign of anxiety. I asked about the problem you would like me to help you with. This stirred up some feelings. The feelings make you anxious, and the anxiety makes you sick to your stomach. Do you see what I mean?"*]

Pt: It's not so bad. [*"Sickness in your stomach is a sign of severe anxiety. When you say your anxiety is not so bad, could that be a way of ignoring and minimizing your anxiety?"*]

Pt: Yes. But that's not what I want to talk about. [*"When you say you don't want to talk about your anxiety, could that be a way of ignoring this anxiety in your body?"*]

Pt: What did you say? My mind just blanked out. [*"That's a sign of high anxiety. Are you aware of feeling anxious right now?"*]

Pt: Oh, my mind does that all the time. [*"Blanking out is a sign of high anxiety. Could we take a look at your anxiety so we could help you bring it down?"*]

Pt: I wouldn't say anxious. I'm afraid. I'm so afraid of what will happen if I relapse. [*"If we come back to this moment, could we pay attention to this anxiety in your body and see if we can help you bring it down?"*]

Pt: Wouldn't you be afraid, too, if your dealer said he was going to get you? [*"I'm sure I would. So, could we pay attention to this anxiety in your body and see whether we can help you with it?"*]

Pt: Okay. [*"Where do you notice feeling this anxiety physically in your body?"*]

Pt: I'm just afraid of my dealer. [*"That's your thought. Since your dealer is not in the room right now, can we pay attention to this anxiety in your body?"*]

Pt: I feel sick to my stomach. [*"That's a sign of anxiety. Where else do you experience this anxiety physically in your body?"*]

Pt: [*Sighs.*] I feel a little tense. [*"So, we see that something about telling me your problem triggers anxiety in your body."* Once the patient's anxiety is in the somatic nervous system muscles, we can ask for the problem again.]

Pt: Yes. [*"So, could we see what the problem is you would like me to help you with?"*]

Pt: I'm not sure what to work on. I hadn't thought of anything. I suppose we could talk about my drug use. But to be honest, it's not a big deal for me. [*"Since it's not a big deal for you, what is the internal problem you would like me to help you with?"*]

Pt: [*Uses a detached, uninvolved voice.*] I was referred here by my sponsor, and he thought you would be helpful to me. He said that I have to get clean or I'll lose my job. [*"You have said what your sponsor thinks is your problem, but it is not clear what the emotional problem is you would like me to help you with. Could you be more specific about the internal problem you want help with here?"*]

Pt: Let me tell you about what happened last night. [*"Before we get to that, what is the problem you would like me to help you with?"*]

Pt: I'd like to move forward in my recovery. [*"To move forward, could you be more specific about the problem you would like me to help you with?"*]

Pt: My previous rehab said I have a passive-aggressive personality, and that may be a problem. [*"That's what your previous rehab thought. If we come back to you, what is the problem you would like me to help you with?"*]

Pt: My boss told me I needed to come here if I want to keep my job. [*"That's what your boss wants you to do. But what do you want for yourself here? What is the problem you would like me to help you with?"*]

Pt: I don't know. Maybe I don't have a problem. [*"So, a man without a psychological problem finds himself in a therapist's office."*]

Pt: Do you think I need rehab? [*"Only you can know if you need rehab. That's why I have to ask you, what is the problem you would like to work on?"*]

Pt: You should ask my wife. She's the one who thinks I ought to be here. [*"Since she is not here, I can't ask her. So, what is the problem you would like me to help you with?"* Block the attribution onto his wife.]

Pt: Well, since I'm here. I guess I might as well talk about the drugs. If I don't deal with that, I'll lose my job. I guess that's it. [*"Are you sure you want to talk about your drug problem?"* The "I guess" shows us that he is not committed to working on this problem yet. Thus, we ask about his will.]

Pt: [*No sigh.*] Sure. [*"What tells you inside that you know you want to do this for you?"*]

Pt: If you think I should. [*"But do you want to for yourself?"*]

Pt: [*No sigh.*] Okay. [*"What tells you inside that you know you want to do this for yourself?"*]

Pt: I know I should. [*"But do you want to for yourself?"*]

Pt: Mmm. [*"What tells you inside that you know you want to do this for yourself?"*]

Pt: I'm here. I know that's what we're supposed to do. [*"But what tells you inside that you know you want to do this for yourself?"*]

Pt: [*Sighs.*] If I don't, I'll lose my job, and my wife will leave me. [*"So, do you want to find out what is driving this drug problem so you can keep your job and your marriage?"*]

Pt: I think so. [*"If you aren't sure, I have no right to explore this problem with you."*]

Pt: I thought you were supposed to explore drug issues with me. [*"No. If you want to explore your drug issues with me, I'm glad to help you. But if you don't want to, I have to respect your wish not to get help with them right now."*]

Pt: Okay. I get it. You're saying I have to work if I want therapy to work. [*"Who had that thought?"*]

Pt: I did. [*"So, do you want to work here to make therapy work for you?"*]

Pt: [*Sighs.*] When you put it that way, it makes sense. [*"To find out what is driving your drug use, shall we take a look at a specific situation where this problem came up?"* Now that his will is online, we can ask for a specific example of his problem.]

Now let's continue the role-play exercise. The person in the patient role should read the following to the person in the therapist role. "That was hard, wasn't it? Holding a consistent therapeutic focus builds the alliance. Now we'll repeat the exercise. As soon as you, the therapist, intervene, I, the patient, will go immediately to the next patient statement. Let's make this exercise feel like a real session. We won't stop for talking. We'll go straight through so you, the therapist, get the experience of processing and intervening more quickly. We'll repeat this until you have mastered it. Then we'll change roles and do it again until I have mastered it too."

Questions to ask each other to strengthen your skills: What did you feel when you held a therapeutic focus without getting distracted by the patient's avoidance strategies? In the patient role, what did you feel when your therapist constantly held a therapeutic focus? What did you feel when you could not distract the therapist? How did this exercise change your understanding of building the alliance? What impact is this having on you when you are aware of avoidance strategies that the patient cannot see yet?

STAGE FOUR: MOBILIZING THE PATIENT'S WILL TO THE TASK

In a therapeutic alliance, the patient declares his will to engage in a task that will benefit him so that the therapist and patient can work together. However, in an insecure attachment, the child has learned to ignore his will and follow the will of others. Thus, the patient may collaborate in the way he was taught: by hiding his will.

Yet, successful therapy requires that both the therapist and patient give 100 percent to the effort. Unfortunately, therapists often try to do therapy without making sure the patient wants to do so. Eventually, the therapist realizes she is working while the patient takes a passive stance. So, we need to assess whether the patient is fully committed to his goals. In the following exercise, you will learn how to recognize when the patient's will is not entirely on board. Then you can mobilize the patient's will to work on his problems to achieve his goals.

Once the patient declares a clear internal emotional problem, assess whether he wants to work on it in therapy. Sometimes it is obvious. But if the patient hesitates, withholds, sounds less than enthusiastic, looks away, or does not engage with you, ask, "Is it your will to look at this problem here with me?"

The patient can respond in only three ways:

1. By saying he wants to explore this with you
2. With anxiety that is too high
3. With an avoidance strategy

Each of these responses tells us what the therapist needs to do next. Let's look at how to respond as the therapist.

Skill-Building Exercise One: Helping When Patients Attribute Their Will to Others

The following responses will test your ability to identify ways patients avoid declaring their will to engage in the therapeutic task.

You will ask, "Is it your will to look at this problem?"

If the patient says, "Do you think I should?" he is attributing his will to you. You can block the strategy by responding, "Only you can know for sure."

If the patient says, "I don't think I want to," he is using the strategy of defiance. You can block the strategy by responding, "Of course, you don't have to look at this problem. But if we don't look at it together, we won't be able to help you with it."

If the patient says, "Am I supposed to?" he is attributing his will to you. You can block the strategy by responding, "The question isn't whether you are supposed to look at it. The question is whether you want to. Obviously, if you don't want to look at it, I have no right to ask you to do something you don't want to do."

If the patient says, "My wife thinks I should," he is attributing his will to his wife. You can block the strategy by responding, "That's what she wants, but if we look at what you want, is it your will to look at this problem?"

If the patient says, "I'm not sure therapy can help me, and it might be a waste of my time," you can respond, "Well, if we don't look at an internal emotional problem you want help with, then you're right: this process will be a waste of your time and money. That's why we need to find out whether it is your will to look at this problem."

If the patient says, "How can I know this will help me? It could be worthless to do this, no offense," you can respond, "You can't know in advance. Either you try it and find out, or you don't try it and don't find out. Obviously, if we don't look at a problem you want help with, therapy won't be able to help you with a problem, and it will be worthless. That's why we need to find out whether it is your will to look at this problem."

If the patient says, "I'm not sure this is something I want to explore here even though you seem to think it would be a good idea," you can respond, "If you aren't sure you want to look at this, I have no right to hear anything more about your problem, much less explore it."

Attribution takes place in two stages. First, if the patient splits off something from himself and says, "It's not me." Then he attributes it to the therapist. Thus, you deactivate the attribution: "The good news is I can't push you." Then you remind the patient of his will: "Only *you* can push yourself to look at something that is uncomfortable." If you deactivate the attribution but don't remind the patient of his will, you will remain stuck. Always do these two steps when a patient attributes his wishes to you.

"That is a lot, isn't it? But as you practice this exercise, you will learn these responses."

Watch a demonstration of how to help a passive patient at HTRBook.com/Video-20.

Practice working with patients who attribute their will to do therapy to other people at HTRBook .com/Audio-21.

As the patient in this role-play exercise, read the following to your partner who is in the therapist role. "I will play a patient who attributes my will to do therapy onto others. You will ask me, 'Is it your will to look at this problem?'"

1. "If I respond, 'Yes', move to the next phase by asking, 'Can we look at a specific example of where this problem comes up for you?'

2. "If I respond with too high anxiety, draw my attention to it and regulate it. Once anxiety is regulated, return the focus to my will.

3. "If I respond with an avoidance strategy, address it, and then return the focus to my will.

"Go ahead and ask me, 'Is it your will to look at this problem here with me?'"

Pt: I know I'm supposed to say yes. [*"The question isn't whether you are supposed to look at it. The question is whether it is your will to do so. Obviously, if you don't want to look it, I have no right to ask you to do something you don't want to do."*]

Pt: Do you think I should? [*"Only you can know for sure whether this is what you should do for yourself."*]

Pt: My husband says I should. [*"But in your opinion, what about you?"*]

Pt: I'm not so sure. [*"If you aren't sure this is something you want to look at, I have no right to hear anything more about your problem, much less explore it."*]

Pt: I'd rather not. [*"And the good news is you don't have to. It's just if we don't look at the problem, I won't be able to help you with it. Of course, there's no law that says you have to let me help you."*]

Pt: Do I have to? [*"Absolutely not. If this is not something you want to explore here with me, I have no right to help you with it. But of course, if we don't help you with it, your problem will continue."*]

Pt: My doctor said it would help. [*"The question here is not what the doctor thinks but what you want for yourself. Is it your will to look at this problem so we can get to the bottom of your difficulties?"*]

Pt: I don't know. [*"Okay. If you aren't sure this is something you want to look at, I have no right to hear anything more about your problem, much less explore it."*]

Pt: This is not actually the problem I want you to help me with. [*"So, we still don't know what the problem is you would like me to help you with."*]

Pt: What is your opinion, doctor? [*"The question here is not what I think is best for you but what you want for yourself. Is it your will to look at this problem so we can get to the bottom of your difficulties?"*]

Pt: If I asked my husband, I know what he would say. [*"But in your opinion? What about you?"*]

Pt: I know I should, but I don't want to. But I also know you want me to, so let me just tell you everything and see what happens. [*"The question isn't whether you should look at it. And the question isn't whether I think you should. The question is whether it is your will to do so. Obviously, if you don't want to look at it, I have no right to ask you to do something you don't want to do."*]

Pt: I'd prefer not to. I feel like you are pushing me to look at this problem. [*"The good news is that I can't. Only you can push yourself to look at a problem or not. That's up to you. If you don't want to push yourself to look at this, I have no right to do so. But then, if you don't want to look at a problem, we could not help you with it."*]

Pt: No. [*"Okay. If you don't want to look at this problem, I have no right to hear anything more about your problem, much less explore it. But as long as we don't look at it together, we won't be able to help you with it."*]

Pt: Should I? [*"The question isn't whether you should look at it. The question is whether it is your will to do so. Obviously, if you don't want to look at it, I have no right to ask you to do something you don't want to do."*]

Pt: This is really my husband's idea. [*"It may be his idea, but this can't be his therapy. For this therapy to work, I have to be working for you, not for him. If this is not something you want to explore, or if you are doing this only to please him, I have no right to hear anything more about your problem, much less explore it. That's why we have to find out if it is your will to look at this problem."*]

Pt: [*Says with a diffident voice.*] I know I need to if I am going to get anywhere. [*"But you don't have to."* Here, we respond not to the patient's words but to the lack of will implicit in his nonverbal behavior. Notice what he says and how he says it. He avoids committing to working together by remaining detached.]

Pt: Do you want to look at it? [*"The question here is not what I want for you but what you want for yourself. Is it your will to look at this problem so we can get to the bottom of your difficulties?"*]

Pt: Let me think about it. [*"Take all the time you want. There's no rush."*]

Pt: Why are you pushing me? [*"I can't. Only you can push yourself to look at a problem or not. That's up to you. If you don't want to push yourself to look at this, I have to accept that. But then, if you don't want to look at a problem, there would be no way for us to help you with it."*]

Pt: My last therapist said if I don't look at it, I won't get better. [*"But that doesn't mean you have to."* When the patient attributes his will onto the last therapist, he may attribute it to you as well. This intervention deactivates the attribution to the therapist in the room.]

Pt: Are you going to try to make me? [*"I can't. Only you can make yourself look at a problem or not. That's up to you. If you don't want to make yourself look at this, I have no right to do so. But then, if you don't want to look at a problem, there would be no way for us to help you with it."*]

Pt: How can I know whether this therapy can help me? What if it's worthless? [*"We can't know in advance whether this therapy will help, but we can guarantee that it will be worthless if you decide not to look at a problem."*]

Pt: Like I said, this is my husband's idea. [*"It may be his idea, but this can't be his therapy. For this therapy to work, I have to be working for you, not for him. If this is not something you want to explore, or if you are doing this only to please him, I have no right to hear anything more about your problem, much less explore it. That's why we have to find out whether it is your will to look at this problem."*]

Pt: I don't want you or anyone else telling me what I have to do. [*"I have no right to tell you what to do. Only you can tell yourself to look at a problem or not. That's up to you. If you don't want to look at this, I have no right to tell you to do so. But then, if you don't want to look at a problem, there would be no way for us to help you with it."*]

Pt: I'm just afraid this therapy will be a waste of time. [*"That makes sense. If it is not your will to look at this problem, we won't be able to help you with it, and then this therapy would be a waste of your time."*]

Pt: I'm not sure I really want to do this, but if you think it is a good idea, I'll just go ahead and tell you everything. [*"If you don't want to look at this, I have no right to ask you to do something you don't want to do."*]

Pt: [*Sighs.*] Okay. The problem is that I get into arguments with people. And this past week, I got into an argument with my boss, and he put me on probation. [*"And is it your will to look at this tendency to get into arguments so you could be in control instead of the arguments taking control of you?"*]

Pt: [*Sighs.*] Yes. Because, if I don't, I'm going to lose this job. And it's the best one I ever had.

Once you have mastered this skill, you can address attributions more easily. Respect the patient's autonomy. She has the right not to do therapy. Effective therapy requires 100 percent from both the patient and the therapist. If she asks you to work under conditions where he cannot succeed, we can remind her that we will not succeed. We also have the right not to violate our autonomy. We, too, can decide not to try therapy if the patient insists that we do it in a way that cannot succeed. If we try to do the impossible, we fail to do what is possible.

You cannot be the engine of therapy. Only the patient's will can be the engine of therapy. Therefore, keep inviting his will until it is online. As long as you block the avoidance strategy and return the focus to the patient's will, your answer will be fine. The goal here is not to repeat the words in the book but to learn the principle guiding those words: the patient's will is the engine of therapy.

Now let's continue the role-play exercise. The person in the patient role should read the following to the person in the therapist role. "Now we'll repeat the exercise. As soon as you, the therapist, intervene, I, the patient, will go immediately to the next patient statement. Let's make this exercise feel like a real session. We won't stop for talking. We'll go straight through so you, the therapist, get the experience of processing and intervening more quickly. We'll repeat this until you have mastered it. Then we'll change roles and do it again until I have mastered it too."

Questions to ask each other to strengthen your skills: What did you feel when you held a therapeutic position without taking sides in the patient's conflict? In the patient role, what did you feel when your therapist did not push you to do therapy against your will? What did you feel when you could not get the therapist to react to your attributions? How is this exercise changing your understanding of the role of the patient's will in therapy?

Skill-Building Exercise Two:
Mobilizing Patients' Will to Work toward Their Goal

Patients often come from relationships where they had to follow the will of others, not their own. Patients from this kind of background have an underdeveloped capacity to declare what they want in relationships. Naturally, that problem happens in therapy as well. As a result, they may go along with what they think you want. They passively comply by following what they think you want instead of following their desire.

Again, this is how patients learn to collaborate in certain insecure attachments. The patient does not do this intentionally or even consciously. It's just her learned relational behavior. Thus, once the patient declares a problem she wants to work on, make sure it is her will to work on it.

Practice motivating patients to work toward their goals at HTRBook.com/Audio-22.

As the patient in this role-play exercise, read the following to your partner who is in the therapist role: "In the following examples, I, as the patient, will offer a potential problem to work on. Each time, offer a possible positive goal and ask whether I want to work together toward that goal. This helps me, the patient, see our task and why we do it: to achieve my goals. Using my statements, try to outline a positive goal and ask if I would like to work on it. I'll begin."

Pt: I'm a people pleaser. [*"Is that a problem you would like me to help you with?"*]

Pt: I didn't want to go see my mother, but I didn't listen to myself, and I went anyway. [*"Would you like the therapy to help you listen to your mother and to yourself as well?"*]

Pt: I feel uncomfortable with this. [*"Of course you do. Would you like help to regulate your anxiety so you wouldn't have to feel so uncomfortable?"*]

Pt: I can't get past that anxiousness. [*"Would you like to find out what is driving your anxiety so you wouldn't have to feel anxious?"*]

Pt: I feel like you are looking for something. [*"I don't need to look for anything because this isn't about my problem or my mother. The question is, what you are looking for from therapy that would be good for you?"*]

Pt: I guess we could look at my being a people pleaser. [*"Do you want to?"*]

Pt: Being a people pleaser isn't working for me. [*"Would you like the therapy to help you to please yourself as well?"*]

Pt: My boss asked me to her office, and then she reprimanded me, but I just couldn't speak up for myself. [*"Would you like the therapy to help you speak up for yourself?"*]

Pt: That guy I told you about approached me at the AA meeting and said he wanted to take me out on a date. I agreed. I just didn't feel like I could say no. [*"Would you like the therapy to help you say no to others so you could say yes to yourself?"*]

Pt: I don't feel seen by people. [*"Do you want to see inside yourself so you have better information about yourself?"*]

Pt: I want to be understood by my mother. [*"Would you like to look into your feelings so you could understand yourself better and feel more in charge of your life?"*]

Pt: I don't feel comfortable talking about this. It makes me anxious. [*"Of course it does. If it didn't, you wouldn't be here. If we avoid what makes you anxious, your anxiety will be in charge of your life. Would you like to face what you avoid so you can be in charge instead of your anxiety?"*]

Pt: I feel very pressed when you ask these questions. [*"I have no right to press you to look at something you don't want to look at. That's why I have to ask you if you want to look at this problem so you can overcome it."*]

Pt: I don't know what to do. [*"Would you like to know what you want so you would know what to do?"*]

Pt: Yes. If you think that is the way to go. [*"But if you go along with me to please me, the therapy won't be designed to please you. Would you like to look at this people-pleasing problem so the therapy will please you and achieve your goals?"*]

Pt: Yes, because all this people-pleasing is getting me into trouble.

There is no reason for the patient to do therapy unless it will help her achieve a goal she thinks would be good for her. Clarify for the patient what we do and why we do it: to achieve her goals. In the past, many patients had to do what other people wanted. In therapy, we ask the patient what she wants to work on for her benefit so her desire to achieve positive goals drives the therapy. Only her positive goals will motivate her to do therapy. Clarify those goals until the patient claims them as her own. As long as you reframe the patient's problem as a positive goal and ask if she would like to work on it, your answer will be fine. The goal here is not to repeat the words in the book but to learn the principle guiding those words.

Now let's continue the role-play exercise. The person in the patient role should read the following to the person in the therapist role. "Now we'll repeat the exercise. As soon as you, the therapist, intervene, I, the patient, will go immediately to the next patient statement. Let's make this exercise feel like a real session. Rather than stop to chat, let's go straight through so you, the therapist, get the experience of processing and intervening more quickly. We'll repeat this until you have mastered it. Then we'll change roles and do it again until I have mastered it too."

Questions to ask each other to strengthen your skills: What did you feel when you kept asking about positive goals for the therapy? In the patient role, what did you feel when the therapist asked about your positive goals? What did you feel when you were asked to declare what positive goals you wanted to achieve? How did this exercise change your understanding of how to build an alliance? How has your understanding changed regarding the role of positive goals in therapy? How will a focus on positive goals change how you work with patients?

Skill-Building Exercise Three: Helping Patients with Defiance

Sometimes, patients have grown up in a family where they learned to comply with the will of others. Other patients also learned to hide their will but in a different way. Rather than declare what they wanted, they opposed what they thought others wanted. Unable to will for themselves, they learned to will against others, what Rank (1936) called counter-will. Of course, if the patient defies you as the therapist, he cannot join forces so the two of you could work together toward a common goal. Thus, you will deactivate the patient's defiance. Then the two of you can finally form a therapeutic alliance to achieve the patient's goals. The following example illustrates how to deactivate defiance.

Pt: I don't want to talk about this.

Th: That's okay. I have no right to ask you to talk about something you don't want to talk about.

The therapist has no right to make the patient do anything. If you argue with a defiant patient, the conflict appears to be between you and him. But the conflict is between his wish to depend and his avoidance strategy of defiance. If you avoid being in conflict with his defiance, he can begin to see how his defiance conflicts with his wish for help. Also, you always lose when you argue with defiance. Either you will lose the argument, or you will lose the patient. So, drop the rope in a tug of war. Stop defying the defiant patient.

Practice helping patients who suffer from defiance at HTRBook.com/Audio-23.

As the patient in this role-play exercise, read the following to your partner who is in the therapist role. "I will play the role of a defiant patient, and you will play my therapist. Block my defiance by mirroring my stance or reminding me of reality. I'll begin now."

Pt: I don't want to stop using drugs. ["*This may not feel like the right time to stop using.*"]

Pt: I want to leave rehab. ["*Wonderful that you are so clear about what you are thinking. There must be some good reasons. Tell me what thoughts are coming up about this.*" *From the patient's point of view, there are always good reasons for a self-destructive action. Find out what those reasons are so you can help him.*]

Pt: You can't make me talk. ["*I'm glad we agree. I have no right to make you talk about something you don't want to talk about.*"]

Pt: I don't want to do this. ["*Okay. I have no right to ask you to do something you don't want to do.*"]

Pt: I don't want to talk in group. ["*Why make yourself do what you don't want to do?*"]

Pt: Aren't you supposed to tell me what to do? ["*I have no right to tell you what to do. I'm just here to help you do what* you *want to do that would be good for you.*"]

Pt: What am I supposed to do here? ["*Nothing. The question is, what do you want to do here for your benefit?*"]

Pt: What do you want? ["*Nothing. The question is, what do you want out of the therapy?*"]

Pt: What am I supposed to talk about here? [*"You're not supposed to talk about anything. The question is, what do you want to talk about for your benefit?"*]

Pt: Do I have to talk in here? [*"No. You don't* have *to do anything. The question is, what do you want to talk about here to get the help you want?"*]

Pt: What if I decide not to talk in therapy? [*"Then the therapy would be useless to you. But then I'd have to wonder why an intelligent guy like you wants to deprive himself like that."*]

Pt: So, what do you think my problem is? [*"I have no idea. That's why I have to ask you."*]

Pt: I suppose you are going to tell me that my drugging is a problem. [*"Only you can know if drugging is a problem for you."*]

Pt: Do you think a bottle of wine a day is too much to drink? [*"Only you can know if drinking a bottle of wine a day is too much for you. That's not for me to say."*]

Pt: I'm here, but I'm not totally committed to this. [*"Thanks for being so honest. You can be as committed or uncommitted as you want to be. How uncommitted would you like to be to yourself and your recovery?"*]

Pt: I don't want you telling me what to do. [*"I have no right to tell you what to do. That's why I have to ask you what you want to do here in therapy?"*]

Pt: You can't make me stop using drugs. [*"I'm so glad we agree."*]

Pt: Do you think I should stop using drugs? [*"Only you can know whether stopping drugs is good for you."*]

Pt: This is weird. My last counselor told me I had to stop using drugs. [*"But both of us know that's not true. You kept using drugs, and you could keep using drugs. That is always an option."*]

Pt: Aren't you supposed to convince me not to use drugs? [*"That's not my job. I have no right to tell you to want what you don't want. If you want to get off drugs, I can help you do that. If you don't want to get off drugs now, we can talk about that. After all, these are your choices to make, not mine."*]

Pt: Well, I've got a drug problem. [*"And is that a problem you want me to help you with here?"*]

Do not defy a defiant patient. Outside of his awareness, the defiant patient tries to have an interpersonal conflict with you. Then he can avoid having an internal conflict over his wish to depend. Avoid being in any conflict with the patient. Instead, let him experience his inner struggle between his wish and defiance. Then he can decide whether to pursue his desire to get help or whether to defy it. Continue deactivating the patient's defiance until his will is online. As long as you block the defiance and return the focus to the patient's will, your answer will be fine. The goal here is not to repeat the words in the book but to learn the principle guiding those words: the patient's will is the engine of therapy.

Now let's continue the role-play exercise. The person in the patient role should read the following to the person in the therapist role. "Now we'll repeat the exercise. As soon as you, the therapist, intervene, I, the patient, will go immediately to the next patient statement. Let's make this exercise

feel like a real session. We won't stop for talking. We'll go straight through so you, the therapist, get the experience of processing and intervening more quickly. We'll repeat this until you have mastered it. Then we'll change roles and do it again until I have mastered it too."

Questions to ask each other to strengthen your skills: What did you feel when you held a therapeutic position without arguing with the patient? What do you understand differently now, as a result of taking that position? In the patient role, what did you feel when the therapist did not argue with you? What did you learn from playing the patient role? Now that you realize that the patient was defying his wish to get better, not you, how does this change your understanding of defiance?

Skill-Building Exercise Four: Helping Patients Who Attribute Their Wish to Get Well to the Therapist

All therapy involves the patient's will to form a healing relationship with you. However, the patient may become frightened when she owns her wish to get well and form a closer relationship. So, she may attribute her wish to get well to the therapist, her sponsor, or the rehab unit. As long as she attributes her will to others, she may fear what they want. And if she fears what they want for her in therapy, she will fear therapy. Then no therapeutic alliance is possible. Thus, we must deactivate the attribution so she can own her will to recover.

Sometimes, patients in insecure attachments are supposed to hide their will when caretakers cannot tolerate a separate will. A patient from that background may hide her will automatically. Thus, we may need to work hard to help the patient form a relationship in therapy based on her will and desire.

Patients don't become well because you want them to. They become well because they want to. In this sense, therapy is an act of faith. We have faith in the patient's wish to become well, even if she cannot express that wish at the beginning of therapy. As you deactivate her attribution of will onto you, she will begin to experience her desire to recover within herself. The patient's will drives all recovery.

Practice a role-play exercise on helping patients who attribute the desire to do therapy to the therapist at HTRBook.com/Audio-24.

As the patient in this role-play exercise, read the following to your partner who is in the therapist role. "In this role-play exercise, I will attribute my will to recover onto you, the therapist. Each time, block my attribution and invite me to own my wish to do therapy. I'll start."

Pt: I'm afraid you will get too close. [*"I have no right to get closer to you than you want me to. So, the question is, do you want to get close to your own issues so you can get to the bottom of your problems?"*]

Pt: I'm afraid all this stuff will come out. [*"You can let as little or as much of your stuff out as you think would be helpful to you. Do you want a little stuff to come out so that you have better information and can make better decisions for yourself?"*]

Pt: I'm afraid you will take this stuff out of me. [*"That's not possible. No one can take anything out of you except you. That's why I have to ask, do you want to let stuff out of you so you have the information you need to feel more in control of your life?"*]

Pt: These thoughts are outside and trying to get in. [*"Do you want to let new information in so that you have more information and feel more in control of your life?"*]

Pt: I feel like you are trying to get into my head. [*"The good news is that I can't. Only you can get into your head. Do you want to know what is going on inside yourself so you have better information about yourself and can make better decisions for yourself?"*]

Pt: You ask me to give you a specific example. [*"I have no right to ask you to look at a specific example unless you think it would be helpful for you. So, do you want to look at a specific example so you can get clearer information about your problem?"*]

Pt: I'm not sure what the program is here. [*"That makes sense because we're waiting for you to say what program you would like to have here in therapy. What problems do you want to work on for your benefit here? What would you like the program here to be?"*]

Pt: I'm giving you blanket permission to dig inside me and get anything out that you think needs to come out. [*"I'm not able to dig inside you. Only you can do that. Do you want to dig inside yourself so you can find out what is driving your problems?"*]

Pt: We talked about my kids, and how I left my kids, and how I've had abortions before, and how people were saying I will feel bad about this years later. [*"That's what people said, but what is the problem you would like to work on here today that would help you?"*]

Pt: My daughter is getting married and has invited me to attend. I'm just worried about what will happen if I go. I haven't seen my kids in years. [*"And is it your will that we help you with this problem?"*]

Always deactivate the patient's attributions of her desire. Without realizing it, she imagines the therapist wants something out of her. In fact, she has forgotten that *she* wants something out of the therapy. Help her own her desires so that she no longer relocates them onto the therapist. As long as you block her attributions of desire and return the focus to her will, your answer will be fine. The goal here is not to repeat the words in the book but to learn the principle guiding those words: the patient's will is the engine of therapy.

Now let's continue the role-play exercise. The person in the patient role should read the following to the person in the therapist role. "Now we'll repeat the exercise. As soon as you, the therapist, intervene, I, the patient, will go immediately to the next patient statement. Let's make this exercise feel like a real session. We won't stop for talking. We'll go straight through so you, the therapist, get the experience of processing and intervening more quickly. We'll repeat this until you have mastered it. Then we'll change roles and do it again until I have mastered it too."

Questions to ask each other to strengthen your skills: What did you feel when you held a therapeutic position without defending yourself? What did you learn by letting the patient have her conflict? In the patient role, what did you feel as you began to own your desires? What did you feel when you could not get the therapist to want something for you? How did this experience change your understanding of building an alliance? What are you learning about the role of persistence in the face of avoidance strategies?

Skill-Building Exercise Five: Mobilizing Patients' Will by Using Their Words

When the patient attributes some aspect of her will, you can use her words to remind her of her desire for therapy, and then mobilize her will to the task. For example, the patient says, "I'm just afraid of the questions you want to ask." Your response will be, "I have no right to ask you questions you don't want to ask yourself. That's why we need to find out what questions you have that you would like answered in therapy." When you intervene, help the patient see her will and desire to do therapy.

Practice mobilizing the patient's will by using her words at HTRBook.com/Audio-25.

As the patient in this role-play exercise, read the following to your partner who is in the therapist role. "I will play a patient who attributes her will onto others. You will play the role of the therapist. Remind me of reality and my positive goal."

Pt: I'm afraid of what you will see. [*"I cannot see anything you don't show me. You are in charge of that. That's why we need to find out whether you want to see inside yourself so you have the information you want so you can make better decisions for yourself."*]

Pt: You keep asking about my problems! [*"I have no right to ask about anything you don't want to look at. That's why we need to find out whether you want to explore your problems so you get the information you need and so you can make better decisions for yourself."*]

Pt: What are you getting at? [*"Nothing, because this is not my problem. The question is, what do you want to get at inside yourself so you could get what you want for yourself?"*]

Pt: Where should I start? [*"I can't know because I'm not you. That's why we have to find out where you would like to start that you think would be good for yourself."*]

Pt: I wish my mother believed me. [*"Would you like to be able to believe yourself even when she doesn't? Would you like to hold onto your mind even when she can't?"*]

Pt: I hide myself from you. [*"That's okay. Because the real question is whether you want to reveal yourself to yourself so you get the information you need and so you can make better decisions for yourself."*]

Pt: People elsewhere in the building are listening to me through microphones. [*"Do you want to listen to yourself?"*]

Pt: I want her to stand up for me. [*"Would you like to be able to stand up for yourself even when she doesn't?"*]

Pt: People on the street are looking at me. [*"Do you want to look inside yourself so you can know what you want so you can make better decisions for yourself?"*]

Pt: My boyfriend should take my side. [*"Would you like to be able to take your side so you could stand up for yourself?"*]

Pt: I don't like that you are trying to get into my head. [*"Actually, I can't get into your head. Only you can do that. So do you want to get in your head so you can find out what you want to know?"*]

Pt: I feel like you can read my mind. [*"Actually, I can't read your mind. Only you can. So, do you want to look in your mind so you get the information you need?"*]

Pt: I feel like you can see through me. [*"Actually, I can't see through you. Only you can see into yourself. So do you want to look inside yourself so you can get the information you need and so you can make better decisions for yourself?"*]

Pt: What do you want me to say? [*"Nothing. The question is, what do you want to say so you can get the help you want?"*]

Pt: People on the hospital unit are always trying to get me to talk. [*"I have no right to get you to talk about anything you don't want to talk about. That's why we need to find out what you want to talk about that you think would be helpful to you."*]

Pt: You are thinking it would be good for me to feel my feelings. [*"Only you can know whether it would be good for you to talk about your feelings. That's why we need to find out what you want to talk about that you think would be good for you."*]

Pt: [*Sighs.*] I guess I should talk about my relationship with my boyfriend because we are about to break up. [*"And is that what you want us to work on?"*]

Help the patient be clear about what she wants out of therapy and why. Continue deactivating the patient's attributions until her will is online. As long as you remind the patient of reality and her positive goal, your answer will be fine. The goal here is not to repeat the words in the book but to learn the principle guiding those words: the patient's will is the engine of therapy.

Now let's continue the role-play exercise. The person in the patient role should read the following to the person in the therapist role. "Now we'll repeat the exercise. As soon as you, the therapist, intervene, I, the patient, will go immediately to the next patient statement. Let's make this exercise feel like a real session. We won't stop for talking. We'll go straight through so you, the therapist, get the experience of processing and intervening more quickly. We'll repeat this until you have mastered it. Then we'll change roles and do it again until I have mastered it too."

Questions to ask each other to strengthen your skills: What did you feel when you held a therapeutic position without pushing the patient? What did you feel when you waited for her will to drive the therapy? In the patient role, what did you feel as you began to own your desires? What did you feel when you could not get the therapist to drive the therapy? How did this exercise change your understanding of whose will drives therapy?

Skill-Building Exercise Six: Responding to Denial through Fantasy I

All of us have fantasies about how we wish things were. But when life shows up instead of our fantasy, we usually find a way to let go of our fantasies and adapt to reality. However, some patients have trouble with the feelings that arise when reality shows up instead of their fantasy. To avoid the feelings of loss they have when they don't get what they want, they may get angry at reality for showing up instead of their fantasy. Then they might keep waiting for their fantasy to happen rather than face reality as it is.

But we can't deal with reality if we don't face it, and therapy can help patients face only those realities that they do not deny. As a result, sometimes we have to help patients let go of their denial. Only then can we help them face and work on a problem in therapy.

When patients argue with reality, therapists may argue with the patient's denial. Then the conflict appears to be between you and the patient instead of between the patient's denial and reality. Do not argue with the patient. Instead, help the patient see how his fantasy is arguing with reality. As he sees and experiences this conflict, he will gradually face the feelings he has to face and then embrace reality instead of his fantasy.

Here is an example:

Pt: Why don't they agree with me?

Th: Because that's not reality; in reality, they don't agree with you.

Practice reminding your patient of reality at HTRBook.com/Audio-26.

As the patient in this role-play exercise, read the following to your partner who is in the therapist role. "I will play a patient, a recovering drug addict who is angry with family members who don't share his opinions about life, drug use, and addiction. I get so angry with them that I think of beating them up. As my therapist, you will remind me of the reality my denial tries to erase. Remember the context: I am angry with a family that does not share my ideas about life, drugs, or addiction. To block my denial, remind me of reality. I'll begin."

Pt: I can't accept it. [*"You can't accept that they don't think what you think."*]

Pt: I can't relate to it. [*"You can't relate to the reality that they don't think what you think."*]

Pt: I don't understand it. [*"That's okay. You don't have to understand their opinion in order for them to understand their opinion."*]

Pt: It doesn't make sense. [*"It doesn't have to make sense to you for it to make sense to them."*]

Pt: I don't like this family. [*"You don't like this family when it doesn't think the same way you do."*]

Pt: I don't have a family. [*"You have a family, just not the one you want."*]

Pt: I can't get my head to accept that. [*"That's okay. Reality will be there whenever your head is ready to accept it."*]

Pt: It's difficult for me. [*"It is difficult when reality is not the same as our fantasy."*]

Pt: Why don't they get it? [*"Because that's not reality. It's not their job to understand things your way. That's your job. Their job is to understand things their way."*]

Pt: Shouldn't they agree? [*"Should they think like you do? Should they be you?"*]

Pt: It would be nice. [*"Yes. It would be nice if reality were the same as our fantasy."*]

Pt: For some reason, I'm feeling sad now. [*"Shall we face this sadness so we could help you deal with reality more effectively?"*]

If the patient denies reality, we can't help him deal with it more effectively. Help the patient see what he is denying. Keep addressing denial until the patient can face what he previously ignored. Only then can we have a genuine therapeutic task to work on. As long as you remind the patient that his wish is not reality, your answer will be fine. The goal here is not to repeat the words in the book but to learn the principle guiding those words: remind the patient that his wish is not reality.

Now let's continue the role-play exercise. The person in the patient role should read the following to the person in the therapist role. "Now we'll repeat the exercise. As soon as you, the therapist, intervene, I, the patient, will go immediately to the next patient statement. Let's make this exercise feel like a real session. We won't stop for talking. We'll go straight through so you, the therapist, get the experience of processing and intervening more quickly. We'll repeat this until you have mastered it. Then we'll change roles and do it again until I have mastered it too."

Questions to ask each other to strengthen your skills: What did you feel when you reminded the patient of reality? What did you feel when you let the patient take the time he needed to face reality? In the patient role, what did you feel when the therapist reminded you of reality? What did you feel when you started to face reality? What are you understanding about denial that you did not understand before? What are you understanding about the therapist role that you did not understand before? Were you hard on the patient, or is denial hard on the patient?

Skill-Building Exercise Seven: Responding to Denial through Fantasy II

Patients will many times exhibit denial through fantasy. Here's an exercise to help you practice bringing patients back to reality.

Practice a skill-building exercise on dealing with denial through fantasy at HTRBook.com /Audio-27.

As the patient in this role-play exercise, read the following to your partner who is in the thera-pist role. "In this example, I will play a patient whose father has sent an email to me on Mother's Day, celebrating life with his third wife just after my mother died. Remind the patient of reality when she uses denial through fantasy.

"Now we'll begin the role-play exercise. I will play the role of a patient who uses denial. As my therapist, you will remind me of reality. I will start."

Pt: Doesn't he get it? [*"Apparently not."*]

Pt: I want him to think about it. [*"You want him to think about it when he doesn't think about it."*]

Pt: Why didn't he think of us? [*"Because he didn't."*]

Pt: He would never do anything to hurt anyone. [*"But he did."*]

Pt: He should get how we feel. [*"A father who doesn't get how you feel should get how you feel. Is that true?"*]

Pt: He shouldn't have sent that email. [*"But he did."*]

Pt: I told my sister he didn't mean anything by sending the email. [*"You told her that an email that meant a lot should not mean anything. Is that true, that something painful should not be painful?"*]

Pt: He should have thought about how we would feel. [*"A father who did not think about how you feel should have thought about how you would feel?"*]

Pt: Yes. [*"Your real father should be the same as your fantasy father. I wish that were true too. But is it?"*]

Pt: Did he really send that email? [*"Did he really send the email he sent?"*]

Pt: I just don't understand how he could have sent it. [*"You don't understand how reality showed up instead of your fantasy. But even if we don't understand reality, it still shows up, doesn't it?"*]

Pt: Now I feel sad. [*Cries. When the patient lets go of denial and faces reality, she feels the feelings reality triggers. And as a result, she can deal with reality and her relationships more realistically.*]

If the patient denies reality, we can't help her deal with the feelings toward her father more effectively. Help the patient see what she is denying. Keep addressing denial until the patient faces what she previously ignored. Only then can we have a genuine therapeutic task to work on. As long as you remind the patient of reality, your answer will be fine. The goal here is not to repeat the words in the book but to learn the principle guiding those words: to deactivate denial, remind the patient of reality.

Now let's continue the role-play exercise. The person in the patient role should read the follow-ing to the person in the therapist role. "Now we'll repeat the exercise. As soon as you, the therapist, intervene, I, the patient, will go immediately to the next patient statement. Let's make this exercise feel like a real session. We won't stop for talking. We'll go straight through so you, the therapist, get the experience of processing and intervening more quickly. We'll repeat this until you have mastered it. Then we'll change roles and do it again until I have mastered it too."

Questions to ask each other to strengthen your skills: What did you feel as you reminded the patient of reality while having compassion for her suffering? What did you feel as you empathized with her wish to make a painful reality go away? In the patient role, what did you feel when the therapist reminded you of reality? What did you feel when you started letting go of your denial? How does this new understanding change what you understood before about your role as a truth-teller in therapy?

Skill-Building Exercise Eight: Responding to Denial through Fantasy III

Since denial through fantasy is common, let's once more practice turning the patient back to reality.

Practice another role-play exercise on dealing with denial through fantasy at HTRBook.com /Audio-28.

As the patient in this role-play exercise, read the following to your partner who is in the therapist role. "In this role-play as your patient, I have divorced my husband, who beat me physically. My mother said she would always support me and would never let my ex-husband into her home. I have just learned that my mother allowed my ex-husband into her home and treated him kindly. In response, I am angry because my mother repeatedly has taken the side of others and not my side.

"Now we will begin the role-play exercise. I will play a patient who uses denial. As my therapist, you will remind me of reality and ask about my feelings toward the mother."

> *Pt:* I feel I don't have a family. [*"But you do. And what is the feeling toward your mother for breaking her word to you?"*]
>
> *Pt:* I want my mother to respect me. [*"But she didn't respect her word to you. So, what is the feeling toward her?"*]
>
> *Pt:* Everything would have been nice if only she had shut the door in his face. [*"But she didn't. And what is the feeling toward her for letting him in?"*]
>
> *Pt:* Is it too much to want my mother to keep her word? [*"Apparently, it was. So, what is the feeling toward your mother for breaking her word?"*]
>
> *Pt:* I just feel such a terrible longing for a good mother. [*"Of course, you long for the mother you don't have. So, what is the feeling toward the mother you do have?"*]
>
> *Pt:* I see other people, and their mothers are kind, loving, and supportive. [*"And your mother wasn't this time. So, what is the feeling toward her for breaking her word?"*]
>
> *Pt:* I want her to keep her word when she makes a promise. [*"But she didn't. So, what is the feeling toward her for breaking her promise?"*]
>
> *Pt:* I don't have a mother. [*"You have a mother, just not the mother you wish you had. So, what is the feeling toward your mother for breaking her promise?"*]

Pt: Shouldn't she keep her word? [*"But she didn't. So, what is the feeling toward her?"*]

Pt: She should not have let him in her house with my son. [*"But she did. So, what is the feeling toward her for doing that?"*]

Pt: I don't want to feel angry with her. [*"But it sounds like you do. Shall we face that feeling so we can help you deal with your mother more easily?"*]

If the patient denies reality, we can't help her deal with the feelings toward her mother more effectively. Help the patient see what she is denying. Keep addressing denial until the patient faces what she previously ignored. Only then can we have a genuine therapeutic task to work on.

In simple empathy, we empathize with the patient's pain or with her wish to deny it. In complex empathy, we empathize with the patient's pain and anger, her anxiety about her feelings, and her avoidance strategy of denial. We empathize with all of her reactions. As long as you remind the patient of reality and ask about her feelings, your answer will be fine. The goal here is not to repeat the words in the book but to learn the principle guiding those words: remind the patient of the reality she denies.

Now let's continue the role-play exercise. The person in the patient role should read the following to the person in the therapist role. "Do this exercise again and notice what you feel as you let yourself empathize with both her anger and pain and with her wish to use denial. As soon as you, the therapist, intervene, I, the patient, will go immediately to the next patient statement. Let's make this exercise feel like a real session. We won't stop for talking. We'll go straight through so you, the therapist, get the experience of processing and intervening more quickly. We'll repeat this until you have mastered it. Then we'll change roles and do it again until I have mastered it too."

Questions to ask each other to strengthen your skills: Life is hard. All of us use denial to avoid painful truths. It is human. What did you feel as you empathized with the patient's wish for a better mother while reminding her of the mother she has? In the patient role, what did you feel as you started accepting the reality of your mother? How did this exercise change you as you empathized both with the patient's pain *and* her wish to deny it?

Skill-Building Exercise Nine: Responding to Denial through Words

People often ignore others' deeds by paying attention to their words. For example, a patient is devastated to learn that her boyfriend has left her for another woman. She explains, "But he said he loved me."

Th: A boyfriend who said he loved you left you for another woman.

Do not argue with her. Simply place side by side what he said and what he did. Empathize with her pain while reminding her of reality. Over time, this helps her see her denial. If we merely empathize with her pain, she will still deny reality, and she won't get better at facing it. Empathizing with her pain while reminding her of reality builds her capacity to face reality. Then she can learn from it and grow.

Practice responding to a patient who uses denial through words at HTRBook.com/Audio-29.

As the patient in this role-play exercise, read the following to your partner who is in the therapist role. "In this role-play, I will play a patient who uses denial. As my therapist, you will remind me of reality: what my boyfriend said and what he did."

Pt: But shouldn't he have honored his word? [*"Should a man who doesn't honor his word honor his word? Should reality be the same as our fantasy?"*]

Pt: He said he wanted us to get married as soon as the divorce was finalized. [*"Yes. A man who said he wanted to get married left you for another woman."*]

Pt: I believed him. [*"Yes. Since you believed his words, it's hard to believe his deeds."*]

Pt: Maybe he will come back to me. [*"Maybe the real boyfriend will disappear, and my fantasy boyfriend will come back to me."*]

Pt: It would be nice. [*"Yes. It really would be nice if reality were the same as our fantasy."*]

Pt: He told me I was the one forever. [*"And you were until you weren't."*]

Pt: But shouldn't his words mean something? [*"His words meant something until they didn't."*]

Pt: I just don't know what to believe. [*"You don't know whether to believe his words or his deeds."*]

Pt: He said he loved me. [*"He said he loved you, and now he loves her."*]

Pt: I can't believe it. [*"I wouldn't want to believe this either. But is it true that you can't believe reality?"*]

Pt: I want him back. [*"Of course, you want his promises back. They are so much nicer than his actions."*]

Pt: Did he lie to me? [*"Or could denial be lying to you when it pays attention to his words instead of his deeds?"*]

Pt: That hurts. [*"Yes, when he left you, he hurt you then. When denial pays attention to his words instead of his deeds, denial hurts you now. Shall we face what he did so that denial no longer causes you all this pain?"*]

When the patient pays attention to what the boyfriend said instead of what he did, she will keep waiting for his words to come true. And that hurts her. We can't help her deal with the feelings toward her boyfriend if she is waiting for the fantasy boyfriend to come back. At the same time, what a painful loss for her! That makes it important to empathize with her loss while reminding her of reality. He hurt her. That is done. But if we can stop denial from hurting her, she can start feeling better very soon. As long as you remind the patient of what someone said and did, your answer will be fine. The goal here is not to repeat the words in the book but to learn the principle guiding those words: help the patient face the reality that fantasy avoids.

Now let's continue the role-play exercise. The person in the patient role should read the following to the person in the therapist role. "Now we'll repeat the exercise. As soon as you, the therapist, intervene, I, the patient, will go immediately to the next patient statement. Let's make this exercise

feel like a real session. We won't stop for talking. We'll go straight through so you, the therapist, get the experience of processing and intervening more quickly. We'll repeat this until you have mastered it. Then we'll change roles and do it again until I have mastered it too."

Questions to ask each other to strengthen your skills: Loss is painful. Think of a time when you wished that your ex-partner still wanted you. What did you feel as you empathized with the patient's wish for the fantasy boyfriend while reminding her of the real boyfriend? In the patient role, what did you feel when you paid attention to what he did? How does understanding denial through words change your previous understanding of denial? What are you learning as you remember the difference between what the boyfriend said and what he did?

A Theoretical Interlude: We Are Much More Human Than Otherwise

"We are all much more simply human than otherwise" (Sullivan 1953). Just because we are therapists doesn't mean we are something other than human. All of us use avoidance strategies to get away from the pain in our lives. None of us are idealized icons of emotional intimacy and wisdom. It would be rare for a patient to use an avoidance strategy that we haven't used. In fact, the more we judge a patient's avoidance strategy, the more likely it is that we use it ourselves. Thus, by embracing our patients, we embrace ourselves and our flaws and weaknesses.

We use words like *empathy* and *compassion* and concepts like "identify with the patient." But what do they mean? They mean that we are all flawed human beings. Every one of us has made mistakes in our relationships. None of us has all the answers. A few letters after our name following graduate school do not automatically convey some imaginary superiority.

We don't have to identify with the patient; we are already human. Becoming human doesn't require extra action. We don't have compassion *for* a patient. Being human means that we already are the compassion, the "suffering with." We are always already resonating with our patients unintentionally, automatically. So where is the problem?

When we feel and bear the pain of our shared humanity, we might avoid it. We may judge or distance from the patient, or treat him like an object to which we apply techniques. Yet, whatever we judge in the patient, we reject in ourselves. Whatever we distance from in the patient, we distance from in ourselves. Whatever we analyze over there, we have not analyzed within ourselves. In short, whatever we refuse to embrace in the patient, we refuse to embrace in ourselves.

When we embrace the patient's avoidance strategies, we embrace our own. And when we embrace the patient's pain, we embrace our own. Thus, forming a secure attachment with the patient requires that we not only accept the patient's humanity but our own. How could we judge any patient's avoidance strategies when we have used avoidance strategies in the past and will again in the future? The more we embrace in ourselves, the more we can embrace in our patients. And, in the end, even an embrace is unnecessary since reality has already embraced our being. Talk to the patient as you would to a friend, another person who, like you, struggles in life, falls, picks himself up, and stumbles forward. "We are all much more simply human than otherwise" (Sullivan 1953).

Skill-Building Exercise Ten: Dealing with Denial

Why do we deny reality? If we see reality, we will have feelings about it. If we don't see reality, there is nothing to feel. In this exercise, you will learn how to help patients who deny reality. Again, remember that you have used denial in your life too. Offer compassion, not judgment. We all have avoided the pain in our lives when it was too much to bear.

Practice working with denial at HTRBook.com/Audio-30.

As the patient in this role-play exercise, read the following to your partner who is in the therapist role. "In this role-play, I will play a patient who uses denial to avoid facing the fact that her abusive ex-husband recently said he wished she were dead. Each time I use denial, block it by reminding me of reality. Help me see how I hope the truth will become untrue. Start by asking, 'What are your feelings toward him?'"

Pt: I'm dumbfounded. [*"How many times has he done this?"*]

Pt: Dozens of times. [*"So, you are dumbfounded after dozens of times?"*]

Pt: Isn't it shocking? [*"Is it shocking when reality keeps happening instead of your fantasy?"*]

Pt: Not when you put it like that. [*"No. We can be shocked only if we see reality and deny it, only to be shocked again."*]

Pt: I wish he wasn't that way. [*"Sure. You wish he was your fantasy instead of reality."*]

Pt: When I saw that note where he said he was leaving, I said, "Really?" [*"Did reality really happen? Could this be how your doubt tries to make reality go away?"*]

Pt: Shouldn't he do something about it? [*"Should a man who does nothing about his problem do something about his problem?"*]

Pt: I keep hoping he will change. [*"You keep hoping the truth will become false. How understandable when it is such a painful truth!"*]

Pt: I don't get it. [*"Of course! We don't want to get reality. We want our fantasy."*]

Pt: I just wish he would stop. [*"You wish reality would stop so your fantasy would appear. I can understand that."*]

Pt: I just can't believe it! [*"You can't believe reality. Could that be why you are failing to deal with it?"*]

Pt: I keep telling him he can't keep doing this. [*"Yet, he keeps doing it."*]

Pt: Don't you think he is wrong? [*"Is it wrong when reality shows up instead of our fantasy?"*]

Pt: Why does he send messages like that? [*"Why does reality happen instead of our fantasy?"*]

Pt: I feel like you are being hard on me. [*"Who wished you were dead?"*]

Pt: He did. [*"And who is denying that?"*]

Pt: Me. [*"So, am I being hard on you, or is denial being hard on you?"*]

Pt: I get it. [*"Of course. Look, I understand why you wish you could make these facts go away. Who wouldn't! But would it make sense for us to face these facts together so we can help you protect yourself?"*]

Putting our heads in the sand never made reality go away. Yet, we can empathize with that wish. Anyone would want that. But we must help her face dangers so she can protect herself. This requires our empathy and realism. The fact that you see reality is not enough; the patient must too. But she cannot see reality until she can see the denial blocking her awareness of reality. That's why you focus on her denial. As long as you block denial by reminding the patient of reality, your answer will be fine. The goal here is not to repeat the words in the book but to learn the principle guiding those words: help the patient face the reality fantasy avoids.

Now let's continue the role-play exercise. The person in the patient role should read the following to the person in the therapist role. "Let's repeat this exercise until you, the therapist, have mastered it. Then we'll change roles and do it again until I master it too."

Questions to ask each other to strengthen your skills: Life can be scary. Think of a time when you faced a danger. What did you feel as you empathized with the patient's wish for this danger to go away? When you were in the patient role, what did you feel as you started facing this danger? What did you feel toward the therapist who was helping you face reality? How might the patient's denial be the most dangerous thing in her life?

Skill-Building Exercise Eleven: Identifying and Deactivating Misperceptions

If the patient misperceives you, she will have a misalliance with those misperceptions. She won't be relating to you but to her ideas about you. For instance, if the patient thinks you want something out of her, she will be afraid of what she thinks you want, having forgotten that *she* wants something out of the therapy. Thus, we clarify her misperceptions. Then she can have a therapeutic alliance with you instead of a misalliance with her misperceptions.

Practice identifying and deactivating misperceptions at HTRBook.com/Audio-31.

As the patient in this role-play exercise, read the following to your partner who is in the therapist role. "The following examples illustrate different misperceptions patients can have. In these examples, you will learn how to help the patient tolerate her wish to do therapy so she doesn't have to place that urge in other people. In this role-play, I will play a patient who attributes her wish to do therapy to others. As my therapist, help me tolerate my wish without attributing it to others. I will start."

Pt: You need to do something about those people in the other rooms in this building. They are listening to our sessions through microphones in your bookshelves. [*"You are worried people are listening to our sessions. Let me ask what might seem like an odd question. Do you want to listen to yourself so you have better information about yourself?" Attribution: other people want to listen to me. Deactivation: do you want to listen to yourself?*]

Pt: I feel like I'm in a fishbowl, and you are staring at me. [*"I have no right to look at anything unless it is something you would like to look at. That's why I need to ask you, what do you want to look at so you have better information and can make better decisions for yourself?"*]

Pt: I'm trying to figure out what you want from me. [*"Since this isn't my therapy, I don't need anything from you. The question is, what do you want from this therapy that you think would be helpful to you?"*]

Pt: I feel like you are trying to take my voices away from me. But I need them. [*"I have no right to take your voices away from you. And even if I wanted to, I can't because your voices are inside you. If you want to keep your voices and they are helping you, obviously, you should keep your voices."*]

Pt: You are trying to control me. [*"I can't control you, and I have no right to do so. That's why I have to ask you if you want to listen to yourself so that you are more in control rather than your anxiety being in control of you."*]

Pt: When I talk with my boyfriend, I can look him in the eyes. I don't know what it is, but when I'm with a psychologist, I can't. [*"Rather than worry about whether you look in my eyes, the first question is whether you want to look in yourself so you have better information about yourself and so you can make better decisions for yourself."*]

Pt: People at the hospital tried to force me to talk about my history. [*"I have no right to ask you to talk about anything you don't want to talk about. That's why I have to ask you what you want to talk about that you think would be good for you."*]

Pt: If you say a thought, it will invade my mind. So, I have to argue to keep all foreign thoughts out that might cause an internal catastrophe. [*"It may be important to keep my thoughts out of your mind. Don't believe something I say if you think it's not true." Prescribe the resistance to deactivate the belief that you want to dominate her mind.*]

We deactivate misperceptions so that the patient can have a realistic relationship with the therapist. In this case, we help the patient be aware of her desires inside herself. Otherwise, she will be afraid of the imaginary desires in her therapist, and then she will be afraid of him. As long as you help the patient tolerate her wish to do therapy without attributing it to other people, your answer will be fine. The goal here is not to repeat the words in the book but to learn the principle guiding those words: help the patient own her desire to get well so she does not misperceive the therapist.

Now let's continue the role-play exercise. The person in the patient role should read the following to the person in the therapist role. "Let's repeat this exercise until you, the therapist, have mastered it. Then we'll change roles and do it again until I master it too."

Questions to ask each other to strengthen your skills: What did you feel as you held your therapeutic position and invited the patient to own her desires? In the patient role, what did you feel when the therapist blocked your attributions? What did you feel as you owned your desire for therapy? What impact would misperceptions have on a therapy? How has your understanding of misperceptions changed as a result of this exercise?

Skill-Building Exercise Twelve: Working with Patients' Ambivalence

Patients who have had an insecure attachment desire a good relationship but fear they will have a bad relationship with the therapist. As a result, they often present with ambivalence. Insofar as the patient has come to your office, he is motivated to change. However, once in your office, he may present as if he has little motivation.

Perhaps he doesn't see how he could change or why he should. Often, therapists try to convince the patient to want what he says he doesn't want. Then conflict is between you and the patient, creating a misalliance.

Instead, when a patient is ambivalent, reflect the patient's conflict rather than taking sides in it. As you help the patient notice his conflict in himself, he will see that he is not in conflict with you. As a result, he will become more aware of his motivation for change. Do not encourage this patient to change. Instead, stay behind the patient and follow his shifts. Let him experience his conflict about change rather than getting into conflict with him. Accept his conflict without asking him to modify, alter, or correct it.

Practice dealing with an ambivalent patient at HTRBook.com/Audio-32.

As the patient in this role-play exercise, read the following to your partner who is in the therapist role. "In this role-play, I will play an ambivalent patient. As my therapist, reflect my ambivalence without taking sides in my conflict. Ask me, 'Would you like us to work on that problem?'"

Pt: I'm not sure. [*"That's okay. You have a problem and are not sure you want to work on it."*]

Pt: Yeah. I'm not sure it's that big of a deal. [*"Even though it's a problem, you're not sure it's big enough of a deal to work on."*]

Pt: Yeah. I mean, a lot of people have problems that don't need therapy. Right? [*"Absolutely. A lot of people have problems that don't require therapy."*]

Pt: So, that's how I feel. I don't feel like working on it. [*"Good that you know how you feel about this. You have a problem and don't feel like working on it."*]

Pt: I can't think of any reason why I should. [*"Even though you have a problem, you can't think of any reason why you should work on it."*]

Pt: Right. So, unless you can think of some reason I should work on it, I don't see why I should see a therapist. [*"Why work on something you don't want to work on? Just because you have a problem doesn't mean you should work on it."*]

Pt: Yeah. I think the social worker is making too big a deal out of it. [*"Even though you have a problem, you think the social worker is making too big a deal out of it."*]

Pt: Yeah. Maybe a later time will be a better time to deal with it. [*"Although you have a problem now, you think maybe it would be better to work on it later."*]

Pt: What do you think? [*"Only you can know when the right time is for you to work on your problems. That's not for me to say."*]

Pt: You must have an idea though. [*"Only you could have the right idea for you. If now isn't the right time for you to work on your problem, it may make sense to wait until the time is right for you."*]

Pt: That could be a long time. [*"That's true. It could be a long time before it's the right time for you to work on your problem."*]

Pt: I know it's a problem, but I don't feel ready to deal with it yet. [*"You know it's a problem, and now may not feel like the time you feel ready to deal with it."*]

Pt: But I won't get over it. [*"That's true, but now may not feel like the right time to get over it."*]

Pt: That sounds crazy. [*"What sounds crazy about it?"*]

Pt: I won't get better. [*"That's true, but now may not feel like the right time to get better."*]

Pt: I thought you were supposed to tell me to change. [*"No. I have no right to tell you to change if this doesn't feel like the right time to change yet."*]

Pt: That's true. Well, I guess I better deal with it.

The patient must want change for change to happen in therapy. We cannot want his want for him. And we have no right to tell him that he should want to do something he doesn't want to do yet. If we did, we would create a misalliance. As long as you reflect the patient's conflict without taking sides in it, your answer will be fine. The goal here is not to repeat the words in the book but to learn the principle guiding those words: help the patient see and bear his ambivalence without getting into conflict with him.

Now let's continue the role-play exercise. The person in the patient role should read the following to the person in the therapist role. "Let's repeat this exercise until you, the therapist, have mastered it. Then we'll change roles and do it again until I master it too."

Questions to ask each other to strengthen your skills: What did you feel when you accepted the patient's ambivalence? What did you feel when you let go of any need that he change? What did you feel when you let his desire drive the therapy? In the patient role, what did you feel when the therapist accepted your ambivalence? What did you feel when the therapist let you take as much time as you wanted? What did you feel when you realized that the therapist didn't need you to change? How does this new understanding change how you understood ambivalence before? What supervision could you offer your partner about tone of voice and manner in this exercise?

Skill-Building Exercise Thirteen: Addressing Passivity

All therapy models have a theory of change in which patients stop doing something that hurts and start doing something that helps. Patients will feel some anxiety or discomfort making that change. Thus, change will require practice and effort. It will take work.

Therapy is a *working* relationship. The therapist helps the patient do the work of therapy: helping patients face what they avoid. And the therapist's effort is necessary but not sufficient. *Therapy works only if the patient works.* If the patient doesn't know what to do to work toward his goals, he cannot progress in therapy. In fact, effective goal consensus and collaboration are two of the best predictors of therapeutic outcomes (Tryon, Birch, and Verkuilen 2018). The therapist and patient work together to achieve the patient's goals.

First, the patient declares a problem. Then he declares his will to work on it. Next, the therapist and patient reach a consensus on the positive goals the patient wants to achieve. Then they reach a consensus on what work they will do to achieve those goals. The therapist describes the task clearly so the patient knows what to do. However, even when the task is clear, some patients take a passive stance.

Several problems often unfold. Therapists overwork when the patient underworks. They become more active when the patient becomes more passive. They become more helpful as the patient becomes more helpless. Therapists try more as the patient tries less. Without realizing it, the therapist tries to give what the patient withholds. But you can give only your 100 percent; you can't give the patient's 100 percent.

When trying to compensate for the patient's passivity and noninvolvement, the therapist becomes exhausted or resentful. The therapist tries to overcome the patient's passivity rather than block it or comment on it. We can forget that our activity reinforces the patient's passivity! If your patient remains passive, review the video of your session to see how you encourage his passivity.

A good working relationship requires both people to give 100 percent. The therapist cannot do it alone. Passive patients don't take a passive stance on purpose. By becoming passive while working toward their goals in therapy, they show us the main problem in their lives.

Passive patients will often invite you to be helpful when they take a helpless position. They will ask you to do what they claim they cannot do. Helping patients take a helpless position does not help, however. Instead, we encourage patients to offer 100 percent of their capacity, no matter what it is. Always remind patients that they get out of therapy whatever they put into it.

No adult partnership works optimally unless both people give 100 percent. That's reality. So, when you address the patient's passivity, remind him of reality: not working toward his goals does not work.

Practice addressing passivity and building a therapeutic alliance at HTRBook.com/Audio-33.

As the patient in this role-play exercise, read the following to your partner who is in the therapist role. "In this role-play, I will play a passive, uninvolved patient. As my therapist, remind me of reality. Avoid telling me that I need to work harder. That's for me to decide. Start by asking, 'Is this the problem you would like to work on?'"

Pt: Yes. But I'm not totally committed to it. ["What level of noncommitment to your goal do you think would be optimal for you?"]

Pt: Well, when you put it like that, sure, I would work on that problem if I could. [*"If you can't, I can accept that. It's just that I can't do this alone."*]

Pt: Aren't you supposed to help me? [*"Sure, if I give 100 percent and you give 100 percent, we can have the best result possible. But if you can only give 10 percent, you would just get another 10 percent result."*]

Pt: But what if that is all I can do? [*"Then that would be all you could get: 10 percent. I can give only my 100 percent. I can't give your other 90 percent."*]

Pt: Isn't there something more you can do? [*"No. I can only give my 100 percent, I can't give your 100 percent. Only you can do that."*]

Pt: How do I stop being passive? [*"That's a good question you are asking yourself."*]

Pt: I don't feel involved in this. [*"You can be as involved or as uninvolved in pursuing your goals as you would like. How uninvolved would you like to be?"*]

Pt: I don't know how to answer that. [*"Take your time."*]

Pt: What can I do? [*"I don't know. Only you can know what you can do, if anything."*]

Pt: What if this is the best I can do? [*"Then 10 percent would be the best you could get."*]

Pt: Maybe it's a reflex I have. [*"If you have a passivity reflex, we would just have to accept it and the 10 percent result."*]

Pt: Can we do anything about it? [*"If it's a reflex, how could you do anything about it?"*]

Pt: Isn't it too much to expect from me? [*"I don't know. Is it too much to expect you to give 100 percent to your goals?"*]

Pt: I've never been a hard worker. [*"And that's okay. Just because you have goals doesn't mean you have to work hard to achieve them. Lots of people make that choice."*]

Pt: I mean, I wish I could. [*"And just because you wish that you could work toward your goals doesn't mean you have to. You can always allow your goals to remain wishes."*]

Pt: I don't understand why this is so hard. [*"I hear that." He takes a passive stance, inviting you to do the understanding.*]

Pt: I should be worth more than a 10 percent effort. [*"But if you don't think you are worth more than 10 percent, why think of yourself differently?"*]

Pt: I can't give more. [*"If this is all you can give, this is all you can get."*]

Pt: I just feel like waiting. [*"You can wait as long as you want before you work toward your goals. That's okay. There may be no rush."*]

Pt: Are you saying I have to work harder if I want to change? [*"I think you just said that."*]

Pt: But what do you think? [*"Only you can know if you need to work harder to have the results you want. If these results please you, why work harder?"*]

Pt: But that doesn't make sense. [*"Why not?"*]

Pt: I won't get anywhere.

Sometimes when therapists practice this exercise, they think the therapist is being sarcastic. They are right to be concerned. Sarcasm would cause a misalliance. We should never make fun of the patient. After all, he is showing us his problem. Given this, why do these comments sound sarcastic? We are feeding back to the patient the logic of his position. For example, "I want a great result without working for it." "If I wait and do nothing, change will happen." His position is irrational and self-destructive, but he doesn't see it. And he needs to see that.

If you try to explain these facts to the passive patient, he will listen passively, hoping that these insights will change him. But they don't. Why? Your activity reinforces his passivity. The more active you are, the more passive he becomes.

Coming back to the concern over sarcasm, if you say these comments sarcastically to make fun of the patient, you will create a misalliance, and the patient will drop out. As he should, if you treat him that way! Thus, these interventions designed to help the patient also require you to change. You must accept the passive patient as he is without trying to change him. Accept his passivity without trying to make it go away. When you intervene, do so from a position of radical acceptance.

When I look in the mirror in the morning, it shows me that I am balding. It does not add any sarcasm. It just reflects reality without adding any attitude. It accepts me as I am while reflecting how I am. This is the stance to take.

Saying the "right" words will not work. Relating from a position of radical acceptance works. Completely accept the patient's passivity without asking him to change or do anything differently. If the need for change no longer comes from you, it can spontaneously arise within the patient. No patient got better because the urge for change rose in the therapist. Patients get better because their desire rises in them. If you can accept his lack of desire without becoming his desire, his desire can rise within him.

As long as you remind the patient of reality—passivity will defeat his goals—your answer will be fine. The goal here is not to repeat the words in the book but to learn the principle guiding those words: help the patient see how passivity defeats his goals.

Now let's continue the role-play exercise. The person in the patient role should read the following to the person in the therapist role. "Let's repeat this exercise until you, the therapist, have mastered it. Then we'll change roles and do it again until I master it too." Developing this skill will require self-mastery. We need to accept the patient as he is without needing him to change in any way. Freud once said that psychotherapy "is a cure through love" (Freud and Jung, 1994). Through radical acceptance, you learn to love reality. Accept his passivity; don't fight it. Learn to accept reality rather than fight it. Once you have mastered this exercise and radical acceptance, switch roles so your partner can master this skill too.

Questions to ask each other to strengthen your skills: In the therapist role, what did you feel as you radically accepted your patient's passivity without asking him to change? What did you feel as you started to accept reality? In the patient role, what did you feel when the therapist accepted you as you are? What did you feel when the therapist did not ask you to change? What did you feel when your desire rose in you instead of in the therapist? How did this exercise change your understanding of passivity? How does this new understanding of passivity change your previous understanding? When you accept the patient's passivity, how does this change your understanding of empathy? Did your partner ever sound sarcastic? What supervision could you offer your partner so that the tone of voice and manner embody the stance of radical acceptance? How does this attitude of radical acceptance change your understanding of the therapeutic stance?

STAGE FIVE: MOBILIZING THE PATIENT TO WORK TOWARD A POSITIVE GOAL

A patient will form a therapeutic alliance only if she thinks therapy will achieve something she thinks is good for her. Yet, often, therapists fail to get a strong alliance precisely because the patient does not have a positive goal.

To develop a therapeutic alliance, first, we find out the problem for which the patient seeks our help. Second, the patient declares her will to work on that problem. But, without a positive goal to achieve, the patient will see no reason to engage in the therapeutic task. The following exercises will show you how to help patients declare a positive goal to work for.

Skill-Building Exercise One: Turning Problems into Positive Goals

A depressed patient has described a problem to work on, but he seems discouraged and unmotivated. Thus, he lacks the will to work on it. In the following exercise, you will turn his problems into potential positive goals to see whether he would be motivated to achieve those goals. Often depressed patients perceive themselves and the world through their depression. As a result, they cannot see any positive goals that motivate them to try something new. Help the patient find some positive goals. Otherwise, he will have no reason to do therapy.

Practice a skill-building exercise on turning problems into positive goals at HTRBook.com /Audio-34.

As the patient in this role-play exercise, read the following to your partner who is in the therapist role. "In this role-play, I will play a depressed patient who offers negative symptoms. Turn each of my symptoms into a possible positive goal for the therapy. I'll start."

> Pt: I just feel anxious. [*"Would you like to take a look at the feelings underneath the anxiety so that you wouldn't have to feel anxious instead?"*]

> Pt: I feel depressed. [*"Would you like to take a look at the feelings underneath the depression so you wouldn't have to feel depressed instead?"*]

> Pt: I feel so tired. [*"Would you like to take a look at the feelings underneath the tiredness so that we could find your energy?"*]

> Pt: I don't know. I feel so powerless. [*"Of course. That's how we feel when we're depressed. Would you like to take a look at the feelings underneath the powerlessness so we could find your power?"*]

Pt: I don't know who I am anymore. [*"Would you like to take a look underneath the depression to find out who you really are?"*]

Pt: I feel hopeless. [*"Of course. That's how we feel when we're depressed. Could we look under the hopelessness, see what it is covering up, and try to find the rest of you?"*]

Pt: I feel afraid of doing that. [*"Of course. Everybody does initially. If you avoid what you fear, the fear will be in charge. But if we face what you fear, you could be in charge. Would you like to take a look under this fear so you can be in charge of your life?"*]

Pt: I feel weak. [*"Would you like to take a look at the feelings under the weakness so you could regain your strength?"*]

Pt: I just am not sure I'm able to. [*"Sure. It sounds like you haven't been able to do this alone. Shall we join forces together and see if we can help you discover your true potential?"*]

Pt: I feel sick inside. [*"Would you like to take a look at the feelings under your sickness so that you could feel healthy instead?"*]

Pt: I have so many physical symptoms. [*"Wouldn't it be nice to know what you feel so you wouldn't have to have symptoms instead?"*]

Pt: What if I can't do this? [*"Shall we take a look and find out your true potential? If we look underneath the anxiety, shall we give this a try to find out what you actually can do?"*]

Pt: I've never been able to succeed at therapy. I always fail. [*"So, shall we work together and see what we need to do differently here so you can have a better result this time?"*]

Pt: We can try.

A depressed patient sees himself and his life through the lens of depression. It's just how a depressed brain works. It's nothing personal about you. He only needs your gentle, persistent encouragement to work toward a positive goal. His depressed brain may need many interventions before a positive goal can arise, so patiently maintain your stance. Do the exercise with this constant tone of gentle encouragement and quiet, if unstated, faith. As long as you turn a symptom into a positive goal, your answer will be fine. The goal here is not to repeat the words in the book but to learn the principle guiding those words: turn a symptom into a possible positive goal.

Now let's continue the role-play exercise. The person in the patient role should read the following to the person in the therapist role. "Let's repeat this exercise until you, the therapist, have mastered it. Then we'll change roles and do it again until I master it too."

Questions to ask each other to strengthen your skills: What did you feel when you kept turning problems into possible positive goals? What did you feel when you maintained your therapeutic position without taking his depression and hopelessness personally? In the patient role, what did you feel when the therapist maintained this stance of gentle encouragement? How is your understanding of the role of positive goals in therapy changing? How does persistence as a form of faith change your previous understanding of the therapist's role?

Skill-Building Exercise Two: Turning Avoidance Strategies into Positive Goals

Sometimes patients present ways they hurt themselves. Of course, this doesn't motivate them to do therapy. If anything, the fact that they hurt themselves merely discourages them further. And if therapists focus only on the avoidance strategy, the patient becomes discouraged and a misalliance results. From an attachment point of view, the therapist criticizes the patient for having a need rather than helping him with that need. Instead, see if you can reframe the patient's avoidance strategy as a positive goal he might want for himself.

Practice turning avoidance strategies into positive goals at HTRBook.com/Audio-35.

As the patient in this role-play exercise, read the following to your partner who is in the therapist role. "In this role-play, I will play a depressed patient who offers avoidance strategies. Turn each of my avoidance strategies into a possible positive goal that the patient might want to pursue in therapy. I'll start."

Pt: I'm too hard on myself. [*"Would you like to be a little kinder to yourself?" A depressed patient will say he cannot be kind to himself, but he can usually see how he could be a little kinder to himself. Always offer a goal that seems achievable to the depressed person. Otherwise, he will get more depressed if you ask him to do something he thinks he could never do. Start with small goals.*]

Pt: I always say yes to what other people want. [*"And would you like to be able to say yes to what you want too?"*]

Pt: I'd like to, but I don't seem to be able to help myself. [*"Would you like to learn to help yourself?"*]

Pt: I'm not able to do good things for myself. [*"Would you like to be able to do good things for yourself?"*]

Pt: I do good things for others and hope they will do good things for me. [*"Would you like to be as good to yourself as you are to others?"*]

Pt: I'm not sure I can. [*"Of course. That's why you are here. Would you like us to work together and find out whether you can be better to yourself?"*]

Pt: I feel like over the past months, I closed down. [*"And would you like to open up to yourself so you can find yourself again?"*]

Pt: I've tried to do things differently. [*"And it sounds like you couldn't when you did it alone. Shall we work together and see whether we could have a different result?"*]

Pt: I feel really disconnected. [*"Would you like to reconnect to yourself so that you can find yourself again?"*]

Pt: I feel really out of touch with myself. [*"Would you like to get back in touch with yourself?"*]

Pt: I cannot like myself. [*"Is that a capacity you would like to develop here?"*]

Pt: I prioritize other people. [*"Would you like to prioritize your needs too?"*]

Pt: I try to meet other peoples' needs first. [*"Would you like to meet your needs too?"*]

Pt: You mean when I am with other people? [*"Yeah, would you like to meet their needs and your needs, too, when you are with other people?"*]

Pt: I hadn't thought of that before.

A depressed patient reveals an avoidance strategy to show you where he needs help. Turning his avoidance strategy into a positive goal shows him how therapy could help. He needs your gentle, persistent encouragement to work toward a positive goal.

Do the exercise again with this constant tone of gentle encouragement and quiet faith. If you express your faith openly to a severely depressed patient, he may dismiss you as being out of touch with him and his plight. So, instead, express your faith through your tone of voice, stance, and persistence. As long as you turn an avoidance strategy into a positive goal, your answer will be fine. The goal here is not to repeat the words in the book but to learn the principle guiding those words: turn an avoidance strategy into a positive goal.

Now let's continue the role-play exercise. The person in the patient role should read the following to the person in the therapist role. "Let's repeat this exercise until you, the therapist, have mastered it. Then we'll change roles and do it again until I master it too."

Questions to ask each other to strengthen your skills: What did you feel when you kept turning problems into possible positive goals? What did you feel when you maintained your therapeutic position without taking his avoidance strategies personally? In the patient role, what did you feel when the therapist turned your avoidance strategies into positive goals? What did you feel as you experienced your therapist's persistence? How did this exercise change your understanding of the depressed patient? What did you learn about the role of patience and persistence in the therapist?

Skill-Building Exercise Three: Turning Negative Goals into Positive Goals for Therapy

Often depressed patients cannot tell us a positive goal they want. Instead, they propose a negative goal, what they don't want. For instance, "I don't want to feel depressed." Negative goals prime avoidance. Psychotherapy researcher Klaus Grawe (2013) said that if the patient cannot offer a positive goal, you should not attempt therapy. No one is motivated to work to achieve something negative. Instead, reframe the patient's negative goals into positive goals that will motivate him to do the work of therapy.

Practice helping the patient turn negative goals into positive goals at HTRBook.com/Audio-36.

As the patient in this role-play exercise, read the following to your partner who is in the therapist role. "In this role-play, I will play a depressed and anxious patient who offers negative goals. Turn each of my negative goals into a possible positive goal for the therapy. I'll start."

Pt: I don't want to feel depressed. [*"Sure. What would you like to feel instead?"*]

Pt: I don't want to feel so anxious. [*"Of course. Would you like to find out what the anxiety is hiding so you could feel calm instead?"*]

Pt: I don't want to feel so shut down. [*"Would you like to look under the shutdown so that you could feel your feelings instead?"*]

Pt: I feel overwhelmed. [*"Would you like to look under the overwhelming feeling so we could find out what it is covering up? Wouldn't it be nice to know what you feel so you don't have to feel overwhelmed instead?"*]

Pt: I don't want to feel stuck. [*"Would you like to see what the stuckness is covering up so we can get you unstuck?"*]

Pt: I don't want to feel so isolated. [*"Would you like to be able to deal with this anxiety so you wouldn't have to be isolated from other people?"*]

Pt: I don't want to feel like a failure. [*"Of course. No one does. Would you like to find out what is driving your anxiety so we can help you succeed?"*]

Pt: I don't want to be always crying. [*"Of course. Wouldn't it be nice to know what those tears are covering up so you wouldn't be depressed instead?"*]

Pt: I don't want to keep screwing up my relationships. [*"Wouldn't it be nice to know what is causing that problem so that you could handle your relationships better?"*]

Pt: I just feel really bad. [*"Would you like to take a look under this anxiety so we could help you feel better?"*]

Pt: I don't want to have these panic attacks. [*"Of course. Wouldn't it be nice to know what is causing them so you could feel calm instead?"*]

Pt: Nothing ever works out for me. [*"Would you like to find out what is getting in your way so that things could work out for you?"*]

Pt: If we can. [*"Would you like us to find out what we can do together here that would be good for you?"*]

No one wants to work hard to achieve something bad. Thus, we have to help the depressed patient find a positive goal for us to work toward. He doesn't wake up in the morning saying to himself, "What are some negative goals I can offer my therapist?" This is just how a depressed brain works and nothing personal about you. Your gentle, persistent encouragement to declare a positive goal will change how his brain is functioning.

Do the exercise again with this constant tone of gentle encouragement and quiet faith. As long as you turn a negative goal into a positive goal for therapy, your answer will be fine. The goal here is not to repeat the words in the book but to learn the principle guiding those words: turn the patient's negative goals into positive goals.

Now let's continue the role-play exercise. The person in the patient role should read the following to the person in the therapist role. "Let's repeat this exercise until you, the therapist, have mastered it. Then we'll change roles and do it again until I master it too."

Questions to ask each other to strengthen your skills: What did you learn about negative goals that you did not know before? What did you feel when you kept turning negative goals into positive goals? What did you feel when you maintained your therapeutic position without taking his negativity personally? In the patient role, what did you feel when the therapist maintained this steadiness? How did you experience the therapist's faith in you? As the therapist, what shifted in you as you maintained your faith in the patient?

Skill-Building Exercise Four: Turning a Lack of Capacity into a Positive Goal

Patients often believe that if they lack a capacity, therapy cannot work. This is merely a legacy of an insecure attachment: "If I have a need, a relationship cannot work." In fact, this so-called obstacle is the opening to our therapeutic alliance.

We need to remind the patient that if she lacks a capacity, we can build it. If she has a psychological need, we accept it and try to meet it. In the following examples, take each lack of capacity and ask the patient if she would like to build that capacity in therapy. Lack of ability is not an obstacle; it's the doorway to the central therapeutic task.

Practice helping your patient build her capacity at HTRBook.com/Audio-37.

As the patient in this role-play exercise, read the following to your partner who is in the therapist role. "In this role-play, I will play a depressed patient who lacks capacities. Each time turn my lack of capacity into the task of developing that capacity. I'll start."

Pt: I don't know what I feel. [*"Would you like us to help you develop that capacity?"*]

Pt: I can't regulate my anxiety. [*"Would you like us to help you build that capacity so you could regulate your anxiety?"*]

Pt: I can't do this. [*"Of course. That's why you're here. You couldn't do it alone. Shall we work together to see whether we can help you build that capacity?"*]

Pt: I can't deal with conflict. [*"Would you like us to help you develop the capacity to deal with conflict in relationships?"*]

Pt: I start to cry when I get angry with my boyfriend. [*"Would you like us to help you learn to channel your anger into healthy self-assertion so you wouldn't have to dissolve into tears instead?"*]

Pt: I'm not able to assert myself with my boss. [*"Would you like us to help you build the capacity to assert yourself effectively?"*]

Pt: Whenever there's a conflict, I just get depressed. [*"Would you like us to help you build the capacity to deal with conflict so you wouldn't get depressed instead?"*]

Pt: I get depressed when you ask about my feelings. [*"Would you like us to help you build the capacity to know and feel your feelings so you wouldn't have to get depressed instead here with me?"*]

Pt: I don't understand why it's happening with you. [*"Me neither. Shall we build this capacity to know your feelings here with me so you can bring this strength to your other relationships?"*]

Pt: I don't know what I feel. I get pain in my stomach. [*"Would you like us to help you build the capacity to know what you feel so you wouldn't have to have stomach pains instead?"*]

Pt: I just think I'm stupid. [*"Would you like us to help you look under those thoughts so we could discover what your true potential is?"*]

Pt: I can't stop this anxiety. [*"Of course. That's why you're here. You couldn't do this on your own. Would you like us to join forces so we can help you learn to regulate your anxiety?"*]

Pt: [*Sighs.*] Yes, because this anxiety is terrible.

No one wants to do therapy if they think they can't do it. Thus, we acknowledge the depressed patient's problem and turn it into a positive goal. She merely needs your gentle, persistent encouragement to declare a positive goal.

Do the exercise again with this constant tone of gentle encouragement and quiet faith. As long as you turn a lack of capacity into a therapeutic task of developing that capacity, your answer will be fine. The goal here is not to repeat the words in the book but to learn the principle guiding those words: turn a lack of capacity into the task of building that capacity.

Now let's continue the role-play exercise. The person in the patient role should read the following to the person in the therapist role. "Let's repeat this exercise until you, the therapist, have mastered it. Then we'll change roles and do it again until I master it too."

Questions to ask each other to strengthen your skills: What did you feel when you kept turning a lack of capacity into the task of building that capacity? What did you feel as you maintained your therapeutic position without taking her negativity personally? In the patient role, what did you feel as you experienced the therapist's faith in your potential? What did you learn through this exercise by not taking the patient's negativity personally?

Skill-Building Exercise Five: Turning Negative Expectations into Realistic Hope

Patients who have experienced a therapy that didn't help often believe that treatment can't help them. Yet, they still suffer and don't know where else to go. Therefore, we have to deal with realistic hopelessness. Unless we can deal with this effectively, they assume that your efforts will fail too. In the following exercise, you will learn how to validate patients' experiences: what they did before in therapy didn't work. And you will learn how to mobilize patients' will to a realistic goal: doing something different to get a different result.

Practice helping a patient who has negative expectations at HTRBook.com/Audio-38.

As the patient in this role-play exercise, read the following to your partner who is in the therapist role. "In this role-play, I will play a depressed patient who offers negative expectations. Validate that what I did before did not work, then invite me to try something different to get a different result."

Th: Is this the problem you would like me to help you with?

Pt: But doctor, nothing has worked. [*"Obviously, otherwise, you wouldn't be here. So could we start by agreeing that whatever you did in your past therapy didn't work?"*]

Pt: Yes. I'm still depressed. [*"Since whatever you did before didn't help your depression, would it make sense then to do something different in this therapy to get a different result?"*]

Pt: Yes. But I don't know what to do. [*"Of course, you only know that whatever you did, that didn't work. So, what did you do in past therapy that didn't work?"*]

Pt: I just talked a lot, and the therapist listened. [*"So, it sounds like you learned that if all you do is just talk, nothing happens. And if I just sit around and listen, nothing will happen either."*]

Pt: Something like that, I guess. [*"When you say that it's something like that, notice how you become a bit vague?"*]

Pt: I guess so. I hadn't thought about it. [*"See, my concern here is that if you're vague, we can't get a clear picture of your problems. Would it make sense to you that we need to be clearer in this therapy if you want a different result?"*]

Pt: Yes. Now that you put it that way. I mean, I just talked about whatever. [*"But we're learning that if you just talk, you don't get better in therapy. So, would it make sense to you that we focus on your problem instead of talking about whatever so you could have a different result this time?"*]

Pt: Yes. But I feel like you are trying to control what I'm saying. [*"I have no right to control what you are saying. But if you do the same thing in this therapy you did in the last therapy, you'll get the same result. Then your habit of just talking will control the result instead of you controlling the result. Would you like me to help you be in control so that habit isn't controlling you and setting you up to have another failed therapy?"*]

Pt: How do I know if this therapy will work? [*"You don't. But we know that it won't work if you do what you did in the past therapy. Would you like to do something different this time so that you can have a different result?"*]

Pt: I'm not sure I trust you. [*"What impact will that have on our ability to work together, do you think?"*]

Pt: Not so good, I guess. I don't know if you are on my side. [*"Even if I am on your side, the habit of talking about whatever won't be on your side. And that habit will keep you from focusing on what is important to you. That's why we need to find out whether you would like to do something different this time so you can have a different result."*]

Pt: Do I have to trust you? [*"Of course not. You can mistrust me as much as you think would be helpful for you."*]

Pt: And then? [*"That's the question, isn't it?"*]

Pt: I don't think therapy can help. [*"I'm so glad we agree. Therapy can't help you if you distrust your therapist."*]

Pt: You're not like my previous therapist. [*"And it sounds like you have a reaction to that. What's the reaction you are having to me?"*]

Pt: I didn't trust her either, but she kept trying to convince me that I should. I finally told her I did, but I didn't really. [*"I appreciate you being so honest with me about your distrust. If you hid your distrust, we would have the same result you had last time. There would be no reason to hope for a better result. Now that you are honest about your distrust, we're already making some progress."*]

Do not fault the patient for engaging in behavior that leads to an insecure attachment. He is collaborating perfectly. He is showing us the problem he needs our help with. Our job is to see why those responses perfectly express his need for help. Patients who have had failed therapies usually do not realize what behaviors might defeat their treatment. Identify and block those behaviors so the patient can have a different result and therapy can succeed.

Do the exercise again with this constant tone of gentle encouragement and quiet faith. As long as you validate that one strategy did not work and encourage the patient to do something different in this therapy, your answer will be fine. The goal here is not to repeat the words in the book but to learn the principle guiding those words: invite the patient to let go of a strategy that did not work and try a new strategy to get a different result.

Now let's continue the role-play exercise. The person in the patient role should read the following to the person in the therapist role. "Let's repeat this exercise until you, the therapist, have mastered it. Then we'll change roles and do it again until I master it too."

Questions to ask each other to strengthen your skills: What did you feel when you held your therapeutic position? What did you learn when you accepted his resistance without resisting it? What did you feel as you maintained your therapeutic position without taking his negativity personally? In the patient role, what did you feel when the therapist accepted your mistrust without asking you to get rid of it? What did you learn about the impact of negative expectations on therapy? What did you learn about your role in addressing those expectations in therapy? What did you learn about distrust in therapy?

Skill-Building Exercise Six: Getting Consensus on What We Do and Why We Do it

Patients often wonder why we do what we do. Sometimes our questions and comments make no sense to them. That's because we haven't oriented them to the task: building capacities in therapy that they can use in their life.

Practice building a consensus on a goal at HTRBook.com/Audio-39.

As the patient in this role-play exercise, read the following to your partner who is in the therapist role. "In this skill-building exercise, as your patient, I will make a statement indicating that we don't have consensus on the goal. As the therapist, use my statement to outline a possible therapeutic task and ask if I would like to work together to achieve a positive goal."

Pt: I get really anxious in relationships. [*"Would you like us to help you with your anxiety here so that you can manage it in your other relationships too?"*]

Pt: Sure. It's just that I can't handle the feelings that come up in relationships. [*"That's why you are here. So, would it make sense to look at the feelings that come up here so you can learn to handle them in other relationships too?"*]

Pt: It's just that you keep asking about feelings. [*"Exactly. And since you have trouble handling the feelings that come up in relationships, would it make sense that we probably have to practice that skill a fair amount until you have mastered it?"*]

Pt: I can't share things with my boyfriend if I think he wouldn't like it. [*"Shall we see if we can help you build this capacity here so that you can have a better relationship with your boyfriend?"*]

Pt: That sounds good. But I've never been able to do that. [*"Sure. You couldn't do it by yourself. Would you like us to work together to see whether we could help you develop that ability here that you couldn't do by yourself?"*]

Pt: When there's a conflict with my boyfriends, I always quit the relationship. [*"Would you like us to help you deal with conflict better here so you could keep the relationships you want?"*]

Pt: I always avoid telling them what I think. [*"Would you like us to help you build that capacity here so you could tell them what you think in your future relationships?"*]

Pt: Yeah. Because I always get depressed. [*"Of course. So, would you like us to find out what is underneath the depression so you wouldn't have to be depressed instead?"*]

Pt: Hmm. Underneath the depression? When I'm depressed, I feel like I have no strength. [*"And would you like to know what you feel underneath the depression so that you could regain your strength?"*]

Pt: Yes. I would like that. But I don't know where my strength goes. [*"So, if I see any mechanism that could be taking away your strength, do I have your permission to point it out so we could help you regain your strength?"*]

Pt: Yes, but I don't think I can do it. [*"Could that thought be underestimating your potential?"*]

Pt: Yes. [*"So, shall we look under that thought and see if we can find your potential?"*]

Pt: I think I would like that.

Just because you think therapy can help doesn't mean that the patient agrees. That's why we always link the therapeutic task to the positive goals she would like to achieve. Then therapy makes sense to her, and she realizes that your work together is always designed to help her achieve her goals. When you ask permission to point out anything that could be causing her symptoms, she realizes why you do what you do: to help her achieve her goals.

Do the exercise again with this constant tone of gentle encouragement and quiet faith. As long as you outline a positive task and ask if the patient would like to do it, your answer will be fine. The goal here is not to repeat the words in the book but to learn the principle guiding those words: get consensus on a therapeutic task to achieve a positive goal.

Now let's continue the role-play exercise. The person in the patient role should read the following to the person in the therapist role. "Let's repeat this exercise until you, the therapist, have mastered it. Then we'll change roles and do it again until I master it too."

Questions to ask each other to strengthen your skills: What did you feel when you linked what you do to what the patient wants? What did you feel as you experienced this therapeutic position? In the patient role, what did you feel when the therapist linked what you do with what you want? What do you understand about developing a consensus that you didn't understand before? How does this exercise change your previous understanding of developing a consensus on how to work together in therapy?

CHAPTER SIX

How to Prevent Dropouts from Treatment

According to Wierzbidki and Pekorik (1993), nearly 50 percent of patients drop out of therapy. In one study, therapists were asked to predict which patients might deteriorate. The therapists predicted less than 5 percent of their deteriorations, Yet, a computer algorithm predicted 100 percent of them (Hannon et al. 2005). Which therapists were best at predicting the cases that would deteriorate? Graduate students. Finally, a review of fifty-three studies found that therapists rarely accurately assessed the quality of the working alliance with their clients (Tryon, Blackwell, and Hammel 2007). The following exercises will help you recognize and address common signals of dropout. But first, let's examine why patients drop out silently rather than telling us they want to drop out.

Sadly, patients from insecure attachments learn to hide their problems. They had to put up, shut up, or get out. Either the problem had to drop out, or someone else would drop them.

In a secure attachment, problems will occur. After all, attachment research shows that even good-enough mothers are in tune with their infants only about a third of the time. However, they also spend about a third of their time getting back in tune with their child.

Patients from insecure attachments don't expect this effort from us. They have learned in insecure attachments that ruptures are either not recognized or, if recognized, ignored and not repaired. Thus, these patients have learned not to reveal ruptures but to endure them. Thus, it is up to the therapist to detect these ruptures and repair them (Safran and Muran 2003).

We need to look for signs of dropout since patients usually will not share this urge openly. And we need to take the first steps in resolving these problems since patients won't ask for help they don't expect. I will never forget a severely disturbed man who yelled and acted out in session and elsewhere. One day I realized a mistake I had made, and I apologized to him. Shocked, he looked at me and said, "That's the first time anyone has ever apologized to me." His comment speaks to how little repair he expected when problems arose in relationships.

If we do not see and address the signs of dropout first, patients will drop out. Thus, we need to recognize warning signals of dropouts to help patients get the help they need.

Skill-Building Exercise One: Identifying Warning Signs of Dropout

Therapists almost always rate the alliance higher than patients do, and they frequently miss signs of a poor alliance. If we don't detect a misalliance, patients drop out. Fortunately, there is a solution.

Before the patient drops out, he tells you through metaphors that he is thinking of stopping therapy (Langs 1989; Raney 1984; Smith 2018). For instance, a patient says, "I've been frustrated with my dentist. He always asks me to come in for another appointment, and I don't want to anymore because it's so painful without enough anesthetics. I'm thinking of quitting him and going to see another dentist."

If we replace the word "dentist" with "you," here is what we get: "I've been frustrated with you. You always ask me to come in for another appointment, and I don't want to anymore because it is so painful. I'm thinking of quitting you and going to see another therapist."

Amazing, isn't it! Patients who quit therapy predict it in the previous sessions. Therapists with lower dropout rates hear these warning signs. Here is another example:

Pt: I was talking to my sponsor, and he really pissed me off. He's so arrogant, I'm thinking of getting someone else.

Th: You mention this sponsor who pissed you off by being arrogant. So, you are thinking of getting someone else to be your sponsor. I know it may seem odd to ask, but just to check in: is there anything I've said that upset you that we should take a look at? I don't want to come across as arrogant. So, if there's anything I said that offended you, I definitely want to know about it.

Learn how to recognize misalliances at HTRBook.com/Video-21.
Practice identifying a misalliance with your patient at HTRBook.com/Audio-40.

As the patient in this role-play exercise, read the following to your partner who is in the therapist role. "In the following vignettes, I, as your patient, will say something about the therapy but in terms of another relationship. Summarize the problem I describe, and then ask how that problem may be happening between the two of us. I will begin."

Pt: I told the psychiatrist I need that pain medication, but he keeps telling me that I can't have it because I'm an addict. Well, this isn't an addiction problem. It's a pain problem. If he doesn't listen to me about this, I'm going to change doctors. [*"You mention you are thinking of changing doctors if your psychiatrist doesn't start listening to you. Just to be sure, I wonder what way I haven't been listening to you that we need to talk about? Because, if I haven't, I really want to make sure I am listening to what you want me to hear."*]

Pt: I really like Bonnie. She is so nice and sensitive in the group. I notice she talks to people a lot more than you do. I feel she is really understanding. [*"I'm glad you like Bonnie. You mention that she talks a lot more than I do and that she is really understanding. Since I talk less than her, I wonder what thoughts you might be having about our work. If there is anything I'm not understanding, I certainly want to know about it."*]

Pt: I went to the NA meeting like you suggested, but I didn't like any of the people there. I look around, and I feel like I can't trust anyone there. Like, I don't really know them yet. [*"You mention not feeling comfortable with the people at NA and feeling like you can't trust them yet. I wonder how those trust issues come up here with me because I couldn't be an exception."*]

Pt: You know that psychoeducation group we're in? Well, I brought up something about my past there, and I could tell the group leader was looking at me weird. You could see she was judging me for my past. Who is she to judge me? [*"You have this sense that the group leader was judging you. Just to check in, I wonder if there is anything I have said here that left you feeling judged. Since that thought happened with her, it could happen here too."*]

Pt: In the therapy group yesterday, I agreed to bring up a problem. I mean, I wanted to talk about it, but once I did, she started asking all these questions. She seemed awfully pushy to me. [*"You mention that this therapist asked a lot of questions and seemed pushy. Just to check in with you, I wonder if there are ways you may be finding me being pushy with you because I have no right to push you to do anything."*]

Pt: In the group meeting, you know the one where everybody comes? Well, anyway, everybody is supposed to speak up, and I didn't feel like it. I was listening. But then they started to give me a hard time for not talking more, like I'm supposed to share my feelings. Well, I didn't feel like it. I just feel like this place is really controlling. [*"You mentioned that people gave you a hard time for not talking, and you didn't feel like talking. I wonder in what ways our therapy may be making you feeling pressured to talk or even controlled."*]

Pt: We were talking about the last rehab place we were in yesterday. I was telling them about how I overheard these therapists talking about some guy there, like he was going to therapy with one of the therapists. And they were talking about his therapy and laughing. At least I knew what really happened there. [*"You mention overhearing therapists talking about a patient behind his back. Is there anything I have done that is making you have concerns about whether I will keep our conversations confidential?"*]

Pt: My sponsor says I don't need therapy. He says if I just work the steps, that's all that I need. [*"You mention your sponsor doesn't think you need therapy. I wonder what thoughts you might be having about the therapy and your need for it."*]

Pt: My roommate is driving me nuts. She won't shut up. She's always asking all these personal questions, and I wish she would leave me alone. I'm thinking of moving out to get away from her. [*"You mention this roommate who is driving you nuts by asking all these personal questions. Perhaps you are having reactions to therapy, too, since I ask a lot of questions as well." Since this patient doesn't like questions, offer the intervention as a statement rather than as a question.*]

Pt: I was talking to my group therapist, and he really pissed me off. He's so arrogant. I'm thinking of quitting that group. [*"You mention this group therapist who pissed you off by being arrogant. I know it may seem odd to ask, but just to check in: is there anything I've said that pissed you off that we should take a look at? If there's anything I said that offended you or seemed arrogant, I definitely want to know about it."*]

Pt: I was so angry at Janet the other day. Here she is trying to tell me how to handle my life, and I didn't want it. I walked out of the meeting. [*"Naturally, you didn't want Janet to tell you how to handle your life. So, you walked out. Just to check in here with me, I wonder if there is anything I've said that made you feel like I'm telling you what to do. If there is, I certainly want to hear about it because that's not something I want to do."*]

Once you do this piece of the work, always tell the patient, "If you have any issues with how we are working, be sure to let me know. If there is anything you don't understand or don't feel comfortable with, let me know so we can work on this together. Does that sound okay to you?"

When you make this link to the therapy, you open a pathway so the patient can tell you about his displeasure with words rather than acting on it by dropping out. If you are open to his expression of displeasure in therapy, he doesn't have to take it out of therapy by dropping out.

As long as you summarize the patient's relational problem and ask if it is happening in therapy, your answer will be fine. The goal here is not to repeat the words in the book but to learn the principle guiding those words: bring problems in therapy out into the open so they can be explored and resolved. Practice being open to the patient's negative feedback. In a good alliance, we want to hear about any problems in our relationship. If you are open to his negative feedback, he will experience your openness to him, all of him. Repeat this exercise until you, the therapist, have mastered it. Then change roles and do it again until the one who has been playing the patient masters it too.

Questions to ask each other to strengthen your skills: In the therapist role, what did you feel when you invited the patient to express what he didn't like about the way you did therapy? What did you feel when you let yourself be open to the patient's criticism? In the patient role, what did you feel when the therapist invited you to reveal what you didn't like about the therapy? What did you feel when the therapist accepted your criticism? What did you learn about listening to metaphors? How does this kind of listening change your previous understanding of listening? What supervision could you offer so your partner can sound and be more open to negative feedback from the patient? How did listening to the symbolic meaning of the patient's statements change your understanding of how therapists listen?

Skill-Building Exercise Two: Learning to Identify Dropout Behavior

Patients at risk of dropping out from treatment often reveal their wish to drop out through misalliance behaviors. Rather than understanding those behaviors solely as resistances, think about them as communications. "It has been against the law for me to talk about a problem in a relationship. But, maybe, if I enact this problem indirectly, you will see the problem and address it." If we can identify and talk about those behaviors, we can reduce the dropout risk and help the patient face what he fears. After all, if he felt no fear, he would feel no urge to drop out.

Practice identifying dropout behavior at HTRBook.com/Audio-41.

As the patient in this role-play exercise, read the following to your partner who is in the therapist role. "In the following examples, I will play the role of the patient, describing some dropout behavior. Identify my behavior and ask for the thoughts about therapy driving this behavior. I'll start."

Pt: Sorry I'm late. I just didn't feel like coming in today. [*"Thanks for letting me know. When patients come late and don't feel like coming in, there often are some thoughts and reactions about the therapy. What thoughts are you having about the therapy that might be making it difficult to come in?"*]

Pt: Could we cancel my next appointment? I don't think I need to come in, and I've got something else to do. [*"Given that you are thinking of canceling the next appointment, I wonder what thoughts you might be having about the therapy that are making you want to cancel?"*]

Pt: No thoughts. I just would like to cancel. [*"I hear you. When people want to cancel, it's often a sign that I am not creating the right environment here for you. That's why I wonder what thoughts and reactions might be getting stirred up in the therapy with me."*]

Pt: Here you go: asking questions! Why are you trying to control me? [*"The good news is, I can't control whether you cancel. You are in complete control of whether you cancel or not. It's just that when people want to cancel, it's often a way to express their concerns about the therapy. That's why I'm wondering what I might be doing here that makes you want to cancel."*]

Pt: I was so tired yesterday, I skipped group therapy and took a nap. I felt a lot better afterward. It's okay as a group, but I really needed the nap. [*"You thought a nap was better for you than the group therapy. Given your ideas about group therapy, I wonder what concerns you might be having about this therapy."*]

Pt: I talked to the psychiatrist today and told him I really need that methadone. I just feel he doesn't listen to me. Is there another psychiatrist I could talk to here? [*"We can certainly consider that because it is important that you feel you are being listened to. Just to check in here, given that you are concerned about people listening to you, I wonder whether there is something I haven't listened to that you need me to hear and consider. After all, if I haven't listened to something, I want to know about it so you feel heard."*]

Pt: I thought of calling to cancel yesterday. I'm just so busy and wiped out. [*"When people think about canceling the appointment, that can be a way they express some reservations about the therapy. So, to check in with you, I wonder what concerns or reservations you might be having about the therapy."*]

Pt: I don't see why I have to be here. I'm doing the steps. I've been clean for two months. [*"You don't see why you have to be here since you're doing the steps and have been clean. Since you don't see why you have to be here, I wonder what reactions you are having about the therapy."*]

Pt: I hate it. I don't like talking about myself. [*"Sure. And I have no right to ask you to talk about yourself if that's something you don't want to do. That's why we need to make sure that you are talking about what you want to achieve, a goal you think would be good for you. Just to make sure we're on the same page, what is the goal you want us to work toward? If we're clear on that, then we can figure out what you want to talk about so that this therapy works for you."*]

As long as you describe the treatment-endangering behaviors and ask what thoughts about therapy might be driving those behaviors, your answer will be fine. The goal here is not to repeat the words in the book but to learn the principle guiding those words: find out the thoughts about therapy that make the patient begin to pull out, come late, or even drop out. Practice being open to the patient. Be the openness you want to see. In a good alliance, we want to hear about any problems in our relationship.

Now let's continue the role-play exercise. The person in the patient role should read the following to the person in the therapist role. "Let's repeat this exercise until you, the therapist, have mastered it. Then we'll change roles and do it again until I master it too."

Questions to ask each other to strengthen your skills: In the therapist role, what did you feel when you invited the patient to express what he didn't like about the way you did therapy? What did you feel as you let yourself be open to the patient's criticism? In the patient role, what did you feel when the therapist invited you to reveal what you didn't like about the therapy? What did you feel when the therapist accepted your criticism? How are these exercises changing your understanding of how to talk about ruptures? What supervision could you offer to your partner to be more open to negative feedback from the patient? How did listening to the symbolic meaning of the patient's statements change your understanding of how therapists listen?

Skill-Building Exercise Three: Practicing How to Begin Healing Ruptures

You cannot heal a rupture if you are not open to its existence. You cannot resolve a misalliance you don't accept. And we need to accept that although therapy helps, sometimes comments or strategies we use do not. In fact, sometimes patients find things we say and do very hurtful. Ruptures happen in all relationships. The mark of a good therapy is not the absence of misalliances but the ability to notice and address them. Like in any good relationship, it is not the absence of ruptures but the presence of repairs that make it work.

As therapists, we are flawed, and we will make mistakes. Likewise, it's impossible always to anticipate how a patient will respond to a given intervention. Something innocuous to many people may have a deeply painful and personal meaning for the patient, given the history of her suffering. It's impossible not to make empathic errors with our loved ones and our patients. The key is becoming more open to those ruptures in relationships so we can repair them. As one of my supervisors once told me, "A patient will always forgive a mistake of the head but not one of the heart." Most patients will forgive mistakes if we try to repair them. But to repair, we must become open to the rupture.

Watch a demonstration of how to be open to negative feedback when there's a rupture at HTRBook .com/Video-22.

Practice a skill-building exercise on healing ruptures at HTRBook.com/Audio-42.

As the patient in this role-play exercise, read the following to your partner who is in the thera-pist role. "I will play a patient who reveals some evidence of a rupture. Thank me for letting you know. Then invite me to say more so that we can heal the rupture. I'll start."

Pt: I really didn't like what you said to me last time. ["*Thank you for letting me know. What did I say last time that you didn't like?*"]

Pt: I don't know if I even want to talk about it. ["*Thank you for letting me know. This must have upset you a lot. If I don't hear about it, I can't repair what happened. Can we talk about this together so we can heal this rupture?*"]

Pt: I feel like quitting. ["*Thank you for telling me first. Telling me gives us the chance to take care of this rupture and see whether we can repair it. Could we take a look at what happened so we could make this better?*"]

Pt: I'm not sure it's worth it. ["*Thank you for being so honest. Whatever I said must have had a big impact. Would you be willing to let me know so that we could heal this rupture?*"]

Pt: I started thinking that maybe you don't care about me. ["*Thank you for trusting me enough to tell me that. Could we look at what I said so we can learn what gave you that impression? That would be a terrible way for you to feel about your therapist.*"]

Pt: I don't feel comfortable telling you. ["*Of course, you wouldn't feel comfortable if you felt I didn't care about you. Could we take a look at what I said so we can see if we can help you feel more comfortable here?*"]

Pt: How can I know whether I can trust you now? ["*You can't know whether you can trust me right now. That's why I'm inviting you to let me know what I said. Then I will have the chance to try to heal this rupture in our relationship. Would you be willing to let me try?*"]

Pt: It's just that I've been hurt so many times. ["*Of course you have. And that is why you are here. And how painful to be hurt here! The difference this time is that we can acknowledge this hurt*"] *together. And if you let me know what I said, I will have the chance to try to heal this rupture. And then we can have a new experience here: a relationship where we can be honest about ruptures and repair them as best as we can."]*

Pt: Other people hurt me, and they didn't care. [*"And so, naturally, when my comment hurt you, you were afraid that I wouldn't care. Would you be willing to let me know what I said so we can try to handle your hurt in a new way: doing it together?"*]

Pt: I'm not used to talking about this sort of thing with people. I just leave. [*"It makes sense to leave someone if you think they don't care. But if you left first, I wouldn't have the chance to repair what happened between us. Would you be willing to talk about what I said so that together we can repair our relationship?"*]

Pt: What if you don't care? [*"If someone didn't care that you were hurt, you should leave that person. But if you left before I found out what happened, I would never get the chance to repair the rupture. That's why it's important that we talk about what I said. Then, from the way we try to repair the relationship, you will be able to decide whether I care or not. Could we try to do that?"*]

Pt: I'm so afraid you will hurt me. [*"Of course, because something I said hurt you last time. And the danger is that you might leave and deal with this alone rather than see whether we could heal this together. Could we look at what I said so we could try to repair our relationship?"*]

Pt: It's hard to say, but last time you told me that I should have left my boyfriend after he hit me. [*"Oh, gosh. You're right. I'm so sorry. I had no right to tell you how you should have handled that relationship. I was wrong to do that. Thank you for letting me know. No wonder you thought of quitting."*]

Pt: You're not angry with me? [*"No. I'm grateful that you let me know when I hurt you so that I could apologize for hurting you. After all, you gave me the chance to repair the damage I caused to our relationship."*]

When patients let you know about a misalliance, always thank them for taking this courageous relational step. Then invite them to tell you what you did that triggered the misalliance. You can repair a misalliance only if they let you know what you said or did. Since they fear they will be punished, they usually hide the rupture or leave the relationship. Either way, we have a misalliance. But when we are open to our patients' dissatisfaction, we show that we are open to the rest of their inner life as well.

As long as you thank the patient for telling you about the rupture and invite her to tell you more, your answer will be fine. The goal here is not to repeat the words in the book but to learn the principle guiding those words: welcome and explore the rupture so it can be healed.

Now let's continue the role-play exercise. The person in the patient role should read the following to the person in the therapist role. "Let's repeat this exercise until you, the therapist, have mastered it. Then we'll change roles and do it again until I master it too. When you practice, speak to the patient as if she is a friend whose friendship you want to keep. Be the openness you want to see."

Questions to ask each other to strengthen the alliance: In the therapist role, what did you feel when you opened yourself to the patient's dissatisfaction? What did you feel when you kept inviting the patient to let you repair the relationship? In the patient role, what did you feel when the therapist kept inviting you to reveal what caused your pain? What did you feel when the therapist admitted causing your pain? What did you learn about how to handle relationship ruptures? What supervision could you offer to your partner to model openness to negative feedback from the patient?

CHAPTER SEVEN

What to Do When You Don't Want to Practice

Everyone runs into motivation problems, whether practicing therapy skills, a musical instrument, or meditation. And everyone runs into the same obstacles. Often, the first obstacle is establishing a new habit: practicing. The second obstacle involves the problems that occur once we start practicing. So, let's start with establishing a new habit of deliberately practicing clinical skills so you can become the skilled clinician you want to be.

ESTABLISHING THE HABIT OF DELIBERATE PRACTICE TO BECOME A SKILLED THERAPIST

Every time you practice a skill-building exercise, you reveal your new identity: an increasingly skilled therapist. When you practice skills, you are the kind of person who becomes an expert. To change who you are as a therapist, change what you do: practice a skill-building exercise. Each time you practice a skill-building exercise, you are an aspiring expert therapist. That's what expert therapists do. Decide to be an expert therapist in that top 20 percent that gets 80 percent of the best results. Then, each time you practice a skill-building exercise and improve, you will prove it to yourself: I am part of that group that practices and becomes more skilled.

Buying this book and doing the exercises shows that you have decided what you stand for: greater skill for healing patients. You have decided what your values are: skill, compassion, and competence. And you have shown what you want to become: a highly skilled therapist who helps a wide range of patients recover. So, any time you wonder if you should practice another skill-building exercise, ask yourself, "What would an expert therapist do? Would an expert take thirty minutes to practice today, or would she waste time on the internet?" If you act like an expert therapist and deliberately practice skill-building exercises, you will become that person: a highly skilled therapist.

Practicing doesn't merely help you *have* skills. Practicing enables you to *become* who you want to be: an expert, skilled clinician. Practicing is how you embody your deepest beliefs and convictions.

To ensure regular practice, make the book obvious. For instance, put a sticky note on your dashboard to remind you to practice when you drive. Or put a note on your computer screen (Practice Now!) to remind you to practice first thing in the morning for five minutes.

And make practice attractive. What if you promise yourself a cup of coffee after your practice? What if you reward yourself after each time you practice? And make it easy. If it seems hard to imagine practicing for thirty minutes, practice fifteen minutes each day. Each time you practice you are building your skills and reinforcing your identity as a future expert. As you get used to practicing fifteen minutes each day, you can take it up to twenty minutes a day. Just remember that the more you practice, the better you get. If you improve 1 percent a day, you will be over 100 percent better in three months! It doesn't take much. Just a little every day will make a big difference over time. And imagine how satisfying that skill, ease, and expertise will be.

Monitor your practice. When I first practiced the French horn, I wrote down how much I practiced each day on a practice card. This way, my teacher and I could see how much I practiced. This helped keep me on track. Today, my running coach and I track my practice: how much I run, how fast, and when. Tracking my practice keeps me on the path to success. Monitor your practice by making notes of it on the calendar. Or you can use a free habit tracker app. Using a practice record can keep you regularly practicing to reach your true potential. And don't forget: amateurs practice less than professionals. That is true whether the field is chess, music, or psychotherapy. So, track your practice to be fair to your potential. Research shows that monitoring your practice will make you more likely to succeed.

Also, be specific. If you say, "I'll practice every day," most likely, you won't. Instead, write down your plan: "I'll practice fifteen minutes each weekday at 12:45 p.m. in my office before my 1 p.m. patient." A specific plan will double the likelihood of your success. If you are unsure when to start practicing, start next week on Monday.

Another way to develop this new habit is to stack it on top of an already existing habit. For instance, suppose you get a second cup of coffee at your local coffee shop each workday at 12:30. You might stack habits this way: "After I get my second cup of coffee on weekdays, I will go to the office and practice skill-building for fifteen minutes." Tie your practicing to something you do every day.

Another way to make sure you practice skill-building is to control your environment. For example, make sure this book is on your desk or in your chair in your office. Then you will see it, and it will remind you to practice.

Also, practice can be hard to do all by yourself. That's why this book is arranged so that you can practice with a partner. Working with a partner committed to practicing makes it easier to practice; you can be accountability partners for each other. Or you can form a skill-building group of fellow therapists so you can practice within a culture of mutual development. Then practicing starts to feel normal because it is the norm of your group. (For more on building the deliberate practice habit, see Clear 2018.)

COMMON PROBLEMS WHEN BECOMING A SKILLED THERAPIST

Here's a look at the most common problems you will encounter.

Self-Criticism

Research shows that we think we are way above average as therapists. This is true of most fields, which is why practice is sobering. You might think, "I thought I was better at this, but I'm having trouble with this skill-building exercise." Our self-image takes a plunge. Everyone experiences this when learning new skills. It's tough to lose chess games, miss notes in music, or botch a shot at a crucial moment in a basketball game. But mistakes are a normal part of the learning process. In fact, mistakes are how we learn. Chess players make a record of their moves in a game so they can figure out where they made their mistakes; then, next time, they'll do better. Musicians often record themselves to learn where they can improve.

And learning from our mistakes gives us the chance to develop our self-compassion. Never misuse a mistake for self-torture. When you make a mistake, don't focus on it. Just do the exercise again. You will not improve by thinking about what you did wrong. You will improve by doing it right again and again and again. Thinking it was wrong doesn't help. Doing it right helps. Just do that.

Don't worry about it if you have trouble with a particular exercise. It only means that you have a terrific opportunity to grow as a therapist. Keep practicing that exercise until you master it. All mastery involves repetition. Ask any great pianist, dancer, or basketball player. They will tell you the same thing: they practiced a particular passage, step, or shot, sometimes thousands of times, before mastering it. So, do not worry if you have to practice a given skill ten times to master it. That's what every expert does to master a craft or art.

Finding Time to Practice

None of us have time for something new because we already give our time to other activities. But whenever something interesting comes up, we always find the time. How? By taking time from something else. It's a matter of priorities. For instance, a musician who wants to become a professional will find three or more hours each day to practice. That means less time watching television, checking the phone, surfing the internet, or looking at Facebook.

We always have time if we take time from other activities. When on vacation without internet access, I had to drive somewhere to take care of my emails. I survived on only thirty minutes of internet access per day! I'm not going to suggest you do that, but you get the idea. You can easily carve out some time to build your skills each day rather than zone out on the internet. Instead of getting lost in Instagram, what if you rewarded yourself with Instagram *after* practicing skills for fifteen minutes? The average person spends two hours a day on social media. Surely you could find a way to carve some practice time out of those 730 hours a year.

Some therapists block out times in their work schedule each week for professional development. Then they can work on skills each week during hours that are not devoted to patients. Some therapists do skill-building exercises while commuting to work or while exercising. The exercises are brief enough that you could practice for just fifteen to thirty minutes a day. The key is to practice regularly. The more you practice, the more quickly you will master these skills.

Motivation

If you wait until you feel like practicing, you probably won't. It's like waiting to feel like washing the dishes. We won't feel like it. We do them because we like the result. Michael Jordan practiced even when exhausted to shoot better in the next game. He didn't wait until he was rested. You will practice more if you remember what you want: to be more effective with your patients.

Don't ask yourself to like practicing. Almost no one does. Relish the result: greater competence. Rather than say, "I have to practice," remind yourself, "I have a chance now to build my skills." "I have an opportunity to become more compassionate with defiant patients in this next skill." Musicians practice every day for the result: to improve until their skills are virtuosic. Don't wait until you feel like it. As the famous slogan goes, "just do it." You will get better results with patients. Keep that result in mind. Practicing is not pleasant for anyone. But competence is wonderful! Plus, you will enjoy helping patients more than before. What's not to like about that? Some of my students have kept track of their alliance scores. As they practiced more skill-building, their alliance scores improved. Those results motivated them to practice more. It's a thrill to succeed with patients that you couldn't help before. Think of practicing as your chance to help your patients more and enjoy more professional success. The time you spend practicing now will save your patients time later because you will be more effective. As a result, they will suffer less and feel better sooner.

And don't worry if you miss a day of practice. Conflicts come up for everyone. Just resume practicing the next day. If you miss a day, then miss the next, you start the missing habit. Practicing the next day strengthens the practicing habit. Focus on repetition, not perfection. The more you repeat skills, the more competent you will become. Get your reps in. The more you repeat an exercise, the sooner you rewire your brain, and the sooner you acquire the automatic mastery you want. You can do an exercise once a day for five days, or five times in one day. You can master a skill slowly after a week or quickly after a day. Your choice. It's all a matter of repeating an exercise enough until you master it with ease. It's not how long you practice an exercise but how many times.

But let's suppose you have a hard time getting started. Then practice only five minutes every weekday and make yourself stop after five minutes. No more. Do that for several weeks, and your motivation will start to kick in so you feel like practicing a bit more. This will get the practice habit going. Every day for five minutes you will practice being the person you want to be: a skillful therapist. It's better to start practicing not enough for mastery than practicing not at all. Even those five minutes once a day will have an impact on your long-term success. Those five minutes may not improve your performance initially, but they will strengthen your identity as someone willing to practice to become a skilled therapist.

Managing Expectations

Learning one or two skills will not immediately change your effectiveness. The more skills you learn, the more complex your understanding, and the more flexible you are, the more effective you will be. It will take time before the results start to improve.

So, be patient with yourself, work hard, and persist, and you will become better as a therapist. Don't worry about how quickly other therapists are learning. Focus on *your* learning. Each day, compete with yourself. See whether you can do a skill more fluently today than you did yesterday. If so, you are improving. And if you keep improving bit by bit, you will achieve your goal. We can acquire a degree in a few years, but no one can become a skilled therapist capable of treating a wide range of patients within only a few years. As Ericsson (1996) has pointed out, expertise takes about ten thousand hours of deliberate practice regardless of the field. Think of becoming a skilled therapist as a marathon, not a sprint.

Discouragement

When we set high goals for ourselves, we will fall short of them at times. A basketball player will miss more shots than usual in a game, a musician will fluff a note during a performance, or a patient will terminate prematurely, believing that you didn't help. This happens to everyone who tries to master an art or craft, and it's a normal part of our growth. A mistake is not a personal flaw; it's an opportunity to learn that next skill at a higher level to reach our goal the next time. Again, expect discouragement when you aim for higher levels of mastery. When we set goals, we often miss them before we achieve them. Identify the skill, and practice it more to achieve your goal the next time.

Self-Compassion

Practicing skill-building exercises, reviewing videotapes of our work, and having supervision expose our weak points. They show us where we can grow. We can grow if we see our weak points, and that's when we can offer ourselves compassion. The more compassion you have for yourself, the more you will have for your patients. It's a win-win situation. Self-exposure, revealed weaknesses, self-compassion, and practicing skill-building exercises to build your strengths—those are the components of all learning. You are not unique. Developing expertise always takes self-compassion, time, and effort. Others have done it; you can too. Your potential is larger than you can imagine if you practice skill-building exercises, review videotapes of your work, and get quality supervision.

CHAPTER EIGHT

Transtheoretical Principles for Effective Therapy

RELATIONAL PRINCIPLES FOR THERAPISTS

To form a healing relationship in any model of therapy, we do not rigidly follow rules; we flexibly follow principles. The following principles can guide your use of techniques, no matter what therapy model you practice. These are just the principles of how good relationships work.

- Do not ask questions to get the "right" answers; ask questions to co-create a therapeutic alliance.
- Techniques are not things we do to an object; they are how we build a working relationship.
- The patient's responses always perfectly express her need for help; our job is to figure out *why* her responses are perfect.
- The patient does not resist you or the therapy but the harmful relationship he fears will occur if he depends upon you.
- Apparent resistance to a therapeutic alliance shows how the patient learned to collaborate by hiding his problems and desires.
- Insecure attachment behaviors are not personal to you; they are impersonal, automatic responses based on patients' past of which they are unaware.
- It is not your job to control the patient but to help her see how certain habits and behaviors control her.
- The patient always does the best he can based on his capacity and conflicts.
- The engine of the therapy is the patient's will, so follow her will, not yours.
- The moment you get into a will battle with the patient, you are the misalliance problem.
- We have no right to explore anything unless the patient has a problem he wants to work on.
- Relate to the patient you have, not the one you wish you had.
- Whatever you resist will persist.

PRINCIPLES FOR ASSESSING COMMON ALLIANCE PROBLEMS

Research shows that no therapist in any model succeeds 100 percent of the time. Thus, all of us run into alliance problems. In fact, some of the most important healing moments in therapy occur when we can identify and resolve a misalliance (Safran and Muran 2003). Since misalliances occur with all therapists in all therapy models, here are some metatheoretical principles for misalliance detection that you can use in any model of therapy you practice.

- Focus on the patient: When you think that the patient has no motivation to do therapy, he often has no motivation to have an expected bad relationship with you. Find out what that feared relationship is.
- Focus on the therapist: When you still think that the patient does not want to do therapy, what do you wish she didn't do? Accept that behavior. Find out why it makes sense to the patient. Then explore it.
- Focus on the patient: When the patient does not give you the answers you want, examine the answers he offers. Figure out how those answers, given his history, perfectly express his need for help.
- Focus on the therapist: When the patient does not give you the answers you want, write down the answers you wish she gave you. This is a picture of your fantasy patient. She is not in the room. Now go back to the real patient you have.
- Focus on the patient: If you are working too hard, what is the patient not doing? How can you draw the patient's attention to this so you can agree on how the two of you can work together toward the patient's goals?
- Focus on the therapist: If you are working too hard, what do you like about being in the rescuer role? Insofar as you are trying to be powerful, how are you actually helpless? Can you accept that?
- Focus on the patient: When the patient tries to argue with you, what is he attributing to you? How can you help him own what he relocates in you?
- Focus on the therapist: When you argue with the patient, you resist the patient. While watching your videotape, say "I accept" every time you argue on the video. By doing so, you will learn what aspects of the patient you are resisting. The next session will shift once you can accept everything you see on the videotape.
- Focus on the patient: When you think that the patient resists the therapy, look at the feelings, issues, and fears she is trying to avoid.
- Focus on the therapist: When you think the patient resists the therapy, examine how you might be resisting the patient.
- Focus on the therapist: When the patient describes you in ways you do not like, write those descriptions down on a piece of paper. Find three ways each of those descriptions fits you. Once you can identify with those descriptions, you will no longer be resisting them, and the alliance can begin to shift.

Conclusion

This book has helped you develop essential relational skills to form a therapeutic alliance in the initial phase of therapy. Of course, any list of skills will be incomplete given the wide range of patients and the range of difficulties that can arise in therapy. But with these skills, your alliances should increase, and your dropout rates decrease.

Now you can see that healing occurs not by doing something to an object but by relating to a person. We don't have to motivate the patient but rather find the motivations hidden within her that she was afraid to reveal. When we think that the patient has no motivation, we forget that she has conflicting motivations.

Since she has conflicting motivations, we must address her conflicts between what she wants, what she fears, and how she avoids what she wants. In this way, you do not create a therapeutic alliance. Instead, you and the patient together co-create a new working relationship, and through this process, you come to know her more deeply.

Yet, no matter how well we think we know a patient, she is always unknowable, beyond our understanding. She is not a concept, an idea, or a theory. She is a person toward which our understandings can only point. So, are you. Just as you learned these skills to develop your potential, your skillful work will also help your patients discover their potential. That is why we do deliberate practice.

Although you will learn many more skills as you develop, these skills will give you the foundation for establishing a therapeutic alliance. Having done that, now it's time for you to become more skillful as you continue on your journey as a therapist. On this journey, we are perpetual learners, always learning from our patients.

Learn about your journey to mastery at HTRBook.com/Video-23.

Teachers' Guide for Using These Exercises in Class

These skill-building exercises can be done by students on their own outside of class, using the instructions and videos in the text. However, they can also be done in your class so students learn both the theory *and* how to put it into practice.

STAGE ONE: PREPARING THE CLASS FOR SKILL-BUILDING

- Show the class the videos that accompany this text so students see how to do the exercises.
- Read the introduction for the exercise in the text to the class. Then they can learn from your prepackaged lecture.
- Next, divide the group into pairs so they can do the exercise.
- Ask each pair to decide who will play the therapist and who will play the patient.
- Then, tell them to start. The person playing the patient will read the introduction to the role-play.
- After half the allotted time, ask the pairs to change roles so the patient is now the therapist, and the former therapist is the patient.

STAGE TWO: MONITORING THE SKILL-BUILDING

Once the students are practicing the skill-building exercises, go around the class to make sure everyone is on task. Common problems occur. Here are some solutions:

Problem: Sometimes, the therapist reads from the text rather than coming up with interventions without the text.

Solution: Remind the students that the person playing the patient will read from the text. The person playing the therapist does not. Instead, the person playing the therapist must figure out how to intervene. If that student has trouble knowing how to respond, the person playing the patient can read the suggested answer from the text.

Problem: Chatting. If students chat, they learn to chat rather than learning the skill.

Solution: Remind them that the patient must stay in the role so the therapist gets the experience of intervening in a real session where the problem keeps occurring. This exposes the students to the real difficulties of clinical work where the therapist must maintain a therapeutic focus.

Problem: Students do the exercise once, then stop to chat.

Solution: Remind them that mastery occurs through repetition. Then encourage them to keep doing the exercise again and again until the time you have allotted has ended so they have mastered the exercise and can do it with ease. Students often do not realize that they need to practice an exercise several times before they master the skill.

Problem: You have an uneven number of students for pairing.

Solution: If your class does not have an even number of students, pair yourself with the weakest student, who will be the therapist while you play the patient. Then you can give that student more time to develop mastery and catch up with the rest of the class.

Problem: A student asks you a question about the material in the exercise, showing a struggle with new information.

Solution: Answer by saying "Good question! As you do the exercise together, see what answers you come up with. I think you will be able to figure this out. And later, we will see answers the group comes up with." Do not answer the question. Instead, let students struggle with their questions during skill-building. Then, during the metacognitive question period, you can invite students to share their questions and what they learned from struggling with them. And if the question is still unanswered, invite the group to struggle with the question. Then the class will do the clinical thinking that leads to good interventions.

STAGE THREE: ASKING THE CLASS METACOGNITIVE QUESTIONS TO INTEGRATE LEARNING

At the end of the skill-building time, bring the group together to process what they have learned. You can use the metacognitive questions at the end of each exercise to guide the class discussion. In particular, you want to find out how this new information has changed their old knowledge to ensure that genuine learning and change have occurred.

Here are some sample questions you can ask to build the students' ability to think about their thinking and their learning:

- How does this new information change your old understanding of (fill in the concept, for example, problem, anxiety, avoidance strategy, alliance, therapeutic stance)?
- What do you understand now that you did not understand before doing this exercise?
- What remains most confusing to you? What do you most need to learn?
- What biases did this skill-building experience challenge in you?
- How does this new knowledge conflict with your old knowledge?

- How does this therapeutic skill differ from how you would have intervened as a layperson?
- How is your understanding not changing? Why isn't it changing? What information might you be rejecting rather than integrating?
- How does this learning through experience in skill-building exercises differ from cognitive learning from reading a book?

Bibliography

Ægisdóttir, S., White, M. J., Spengler, P. M., Maugherman, A. S., Anderson, L. A., Cook, R. S., and Rush, J. D. (2006). The meta-analysis of clinical judgment project: Fifty-six years of accumulated research on clinical versus statistical prediction. *The Counseling Psychologist, 34,* 341–382. http://dx.doi.org/10.1177/0011000005285875

Abbass, A. (2015). *Reaching through resistance.* Seven Leaves Press.

Bailey, R. J., and Ogles, B. M. (2019). Common factors as a therapeutic approach: What is required? *Practice Innovations, 4*(4), 241–254. https://doi.org/10.1037/pri0000100

Baldwin, S. A., and Imel, Z. E. (2013). Therapist effects: findings and methods. In M. J. Lambert, (Ed.), *Bergin and Garfield's handbook of psychotherapy and behavior change* (5th ed.), pp. 258–297). Wiley.

Barlow, D. H. (2010). Negative effects from psychological treatments: A perspective. *American Psychologist, 65*(1), 13.

Barsuk, J., Cohen, E., Caprio, T., McGaghie, Simuni, T., and Wayne D. (2012). Simulation-based education with mastery learning improves residents' lumbar puncture skills. *Neurology 79*(2):132–137. https://doi.org/10.1212/WNL.0b013e31825dd39d

Barsuk, J., McGaghie, W., Cohen, E., O'Leary, K., and Wayne, D. (2009). Simulation-based mastery learning reduces complications during central venous catheter insertion in a medical intensive care unit. *Critical Care Medicine, 37*(10), 2697–2701.

Beck, A. (1967). *The diagnosis and management of depression.* University of Pennsylvania Press.

Beck, J., and Beck, A. (2020). *Cognitive behavior therapy: Basics and beyond* (3rd ed.). Guilford Press.

Bell R., Jr., Biester, T., Tabuenca, A., Rhodes, R., Cofer, J., Britt, L, Lewis, F. Jr., (2009). Operative experience of residents in U.S. surgery programs: A gap between expectation and experience. *Annals of Surgery, 249,* 719–724.

Benish, S., Imel, Z., and Wampold, B. (2008). The relative efficacy of bona fide psychotherapies for treating post-traumatic stress disorder: A meta-analysis of direct comparisons. *Clinical Psychology Review, 28*(5), 746–758. https://doi.org/10.1016/j.cpr.2007.10.005

Benjamin, L. (2015). The arts, crafts, and sciences of psychotherapy. *Journal of Clinical Psychology, 71*(11), 1070–1082.

Bordin, E. S. (1994). Theory and research on the therapeutic working alliance: New directions. In A. Horvath & L. Greenberg (Eds.), *The working alliance: Theory, research, and practice* (pp. 13–37). Wiley.

Bowlby, J. (1969). *Attachment: Attachment and loss. Vol. 1.* : Basic Books.

Bowlby, J. (1973). *Attachment: Separation. Vol. 2.* Basic Books.

Bowlby, J. (1980). *Attachment and loss. Vol. 3.* Basic Books.

Burnham, D., Gladstone, A., and Gibson, R. (1969). *Schizophrenia and the need-fear dilemma.* New York: International Universities Press.

Castonaguay, L., and Hill, C. E. (2017). *How and why are some therapists better than others? Understanding therapist effects.* APA Press.

Chow, D., Miller, S., Seidel, J., Kane, R., Thornton, J., and Andrews, W. (2015). The role of deliberate practice in the development of highly effective psychotherapists. *Psychotherapy, 52*(3), 337–345.

Clear, J. (2018). *Atomic Habits: An easy and proven way to build good habits and break bad ones.* Penguin.

Cohen, E., Barsuk, J., Moazed, F., Caprio, T., Didwania, A., McGaghie, W., and Wayne, D. (2013). Making July safer: Mastery learning of clinical skills during intern boot camp. *Academic Medicine, 88,* 233–239.

Davanloo, H. (2002–2004). Personal communication.

Duncan, B. (2010). *On becoming a better therapist.* APA Press.

Ellis, M. V., Berger, L., Hanus, A. E., Ayala, E. E., Swords, B. A., and Siembor, M. (2014). Inadequate and harmful clinical supervision: Testing a revised framework and assessing occurrence. *The Counseling Psychologist, 42* (4), 434–472. doi.org/10.1177/0011000013508656

Ericsson, K. (Ed.) (1996). *The road to excellence: The acquisition of expert performance in the arts and sciences, sports, and games.* Laurence Erlbaum Associates.

Ericsson, K. (2008). Deliberate practice and acquisition of expert performance: A general overview. *Academic Emergency Medicine, 15*(11), 988–994.

Ericsson K. (2014). Necessity is the mother of invention: Video recording firsthand perspectives of critical medical procedures to make simulated training more effective. *Academic Medicine, 89,* 17–20.

Ericsson, K., Hoffman, R., Kosbelt, A., and Williams, A. (Eds.). (2018). *The Cambridge handbook of expertise and expert performance.* Cambridge University Press.

Evans, F. (1996). *Harry Stack Sullivan: Interpersonal theory and therapy.* Routledge.

Frederickson, J. (2013). *Co-creating change: Effective dynamic therapy techniques.* Seven Leaves Press.

Frederickson, J. (2021). *Co-creating safety: Healing the fragile patient*. Seven Leaves Press.

Frederickson, J., Dendooven, B., Abbass, A., Solbakken, O., and Rousmaniere, T. (2019). ISTDP informed treatment within an inpatient drug rehabilitation facility. *Journal of Addictive Diseases, 37*, 195–201. doi.org/10.1080/10550887.2019.1658513

Freud, S. (1923). *The ego and the id and other works*. The Standard Edition of the Complete Psychological Works of Sigmund Freud. XIX. Hogarth Press.

Freud, S., and Jung, C. (1994). Letter to Jung, 1906. *Freud/Jung letters* (W. McGuire, Ed.). Princeton University Press.

Garfield, S. L. (1997). The therapist as a neglected variable in psychotherapy research. *Clinical Psychology: Science and Practice, 4*, 40–43.

Gerger, H., Munder, T., and Barth, G. (2014). Specific and nonspecific psychological interventions for PTSD symptoms: A meta-analysis with problem complexity as a moderator. *Journal of Clinical Psychology 70*(7), 601–15. https://doi.org/10.1002/jclp.22059

Goldberg, S., Rousmaniere, T., Miller, S., Whipple, J., Nielsen, S., Hoyt, W., and Wampold, B. (2016). Do psychotherapists improve with time and experience? A longitudinal analysis of outcomes in a clinical setting. *Journal of Counseling Psychology, 63*(1), 1.

Grawe, K. (2013). *Neuropsychotherapy: How the neurosciences inform effective psychotherapy*. Psychology Press.

Hannan, C., Lambert, M. J., Harmon, C., Nielsen, S. L., Smart, D. W., Shimokawa, K., and Sutton S. W. (2005). A lab test and algorithms for identifying clients at risk for treatment failure. *Journal of Clinical Psychology, 61*(2), 155–163. doi.org/10.1002/jclp.20108

Hartmann, H. (1965). *Ego psychology: Selected papers in psychoanalytic theory*. International Universities Press.

Horvath, A. O., Del Re, A. C., Fluckiger, C., and Symmonds, D. (2011). The alliance in adult psychotherapy. In J. C. Norcross (Ed.), *Psychotherapy relationships that work* (2nd ed.). Oxford University Press.

Joorabchi, A., and Devries, L. (1996) The evaluation of clinical competence: The gap between expectations and performance. *Pediatrics, 97*, 179–184.

Kraus, D. R., Castonguay, L., Boswell, J. F., Nordberg, S. S., and Hayes, J. A. (2011). Therapist effectiveness: Implications for accountability and patient care. *Psychotherapy Research, 21*(3), 267–276. doi.org/10.1080/10503307.2011.563249

Kyser, K., Lu, X., Santillan, D., Santillan, M., Caughey, A., Wilson, M., and Cram, P. (2014). Forceps deliveries in teaching and non-teaching hospitals: Are volumes sufficient for physicians to acquire and maintain competence? *Academic Medicine, 89*, 71–76.

Ladany, N. (2007). Does psychotherapy training matter? Maybe not. *Psychotherapy: Theory, Research, Practice, Training, 44*(4), 392.

Lambert, M. (2013). The efficacy and effectiveness of psychotherapy. In M. J. Lambert (Ed.), *Bergin and Garfield's handbook of psychotherapy and behavior change* (6th ed., pp. 169–218). Wiley.

Lambert, M. J., and Ogles, B. M. (2004). The efficacy and effectiveness of psychotherapy. In M. J. Lambert (Ed.), *Bergin and Garfield's handbook of psychotherapy and behavior change.* (5th ed., pp. 139–153). Wiley.

Langs, R. (1989). *The technique of psychoanalytic psychotherapy, Vol. 1: Initial contact, theoretical framework, understanding the patient's communications, the therapist's interventions.* Jason Aronson.

Luborsky, L., McLellan, A., Diguer, L., Woody, G., and Seligman, D. (1997). The psychotherapist matters: Comparison of outcomes across twenty-two therapists and seven patient samples. *Clinical Psychology: Science and Practice, 4,* 53–65.

Lundh, L. (2014). The search for common factors in psychotherapy: Two theoretical models, with different empirical implications. *Psychology and Behavioral Sciences, 3,* 131–150. http://dx.doi.org/10.11648/j.pbs.20140305.11

Lyons-Ruth, K. (1996). Attachment relationships among children with aggressive behavior problems: The role of disorganized early attachment patterns. *Journal of Consulting and Clinical Psychology, 64*(1), 64–73. https://doi.org/10.1037/0022-006X.64.1.64.

Lypson, M., Frohna, J., Gruppen, L., and Wooliscroft, J. (2004). Identifying residents' competencies at baseline: Assessing the gaps. *Academic Medicine, 79,* 564–570.

Martin, D., Garske, J., and Davis, K. (2000). Relation of the therapeutic alliance with outcome and other variables: A meta-analysis and review. *Journal of Consulting and Clinical Psychology, 68,* 438–450.

McGaghie, W., Issenberg, S., Barsuk, J., and Wayne, D. (2014). A critical review of simulation-based mastery learning with translational outcomes. *Medical Education in Review, 48*(4), 375–385. https://doi.org/10.1111/medu.12391

McGaghie, W., and Kristopaitis, T. (2015). Deliberate practice and mastery learning: Origins of expert medical performance. In J. Cleland and S. Durney (Eds.), *Researching medical education,* (pp. 219–230). Wiley.

Miller, R., and Rollnick, S. (2012). *Motivational interviewing: Helping people change (3rd Edition).* Guilford.

Miller, S., and Hubble, M. (2011). The road to mastery. *Psychotherapy Networker, 32,* 22–60.

Miller, S., Hubble, M., Chow, D., and Seidel, J. (2013). The outcome of psychotherapy: Yesterday, today, and tomorrow. *Psychotherapy, 50*(1), 88–97.

Miller, S., Hubble, M., and Duncan, B. (2007). Supershrinks. *Psychotherapy Networker, 31,* 26–35.

Minami, T., Brown, G., McCulloch, J., and Bolstrom, B. J. (2012). Benchmarking therapists: Furthering the benchmarking method in its application to clinical practice. *Quality and Quantity, 46*(6), 1699–1708. doi.org/10.1007/s11135-011-9548-4

Norcross, J. C. (2002). *Psychotherapy relationships that work: Therapist contributions and responsiveness to patients.* Oxford Universities Press.

Norcross, J., and Lambert, M. (2018). Psychotherapy relationships that work III. *Psychotherapy, 55*(4), 303–315. http://dx.doi.org/10.1037/pst0000193

Norcross, J., and Wampold, B. (2019). Relationships and responsiveness in the psychological treatment of trauma: The tragedy of the APA Clinical Practice Guideline. *Psychotherapy, 56*(3), 391–399. https://doi.org/10.1037/pst0000228

Nyman, S., Nafzinger, M., and Smith, T. (2011). Client outcomes across counselor training level with a multi-tiered supervision model. *Journal of Counseling and Development, 88*, 204–209.

Okiishi, J., Lambert, M. J., Nielsen, S. L., and Ogles, B. M. (2003). Waiting for supershrink: An empirical analysis of therapist effects. *Clinical Psychology and Psychotherapy, 10*(6), 361–373. doi.org/10.1002/cpp.383

Orlinsky, D. and Ronnestad, M. (2005). *How psychotherapists develop: Therapeutic work and professional development.* American Psychological Association.

Porges, S. (2011). *The polyvagal theory: Neurophysiological foundations of emotions, attachment, communication, and self-regulation.* Norton.

Post, J., and Semrad, E. (1965). The psychosis-prone personality. *Psychiatric Services, 16*(2), 81–84. https://doi.org/10.1176/ps.16.2.81

Raney, J. (Ed.)(1984). *Listening and interpreting: The challenge of the work of Robert Langs.* Jason Aronson.

Rank, O. (1936). *Will therapy.* Norton.

Ricks, D. F. (1974). Supershrinks: Methods of therapists judged successful on the basis of adult outcomes of adolescent patients. In D. F. Ricks, M. Roff, and A. Thomas (Eds.), *Life history research in psychopathology* (pp. 288–308). University of Minnesota Press.

Robertson, R. Biaggioni, I., Burnstock, G., Low, P. A., and Paton, J. F. R. (Eds.). (2004). *Primer on the autonomic nervous system.* Academic Press.

Rousmaniere, T. (2016). *Deliberate practice: A guide to improving clinical effectiveness.* Routledge.

Safran, J., and Muran, C. (2003). *Negotiating the treatment alliance: a relational treatment guide.* Guilford.

Saxon, D., and Barkham, M. (2012). Patterns of therapist variability: Therapist effects and the contribution of patient severity and risk. *Journal of Consulting and Clinical Psychology, 80*, 535–546.

Schauenberg, H., Buchheim, A., Beckh, K., Nolte, T., Brehnk-Franz, K., Leichsenring, F., Strack, M., and Dinger, U. (2010). The influence of psychodynamically oriented therapists' attachment representations on outcome and alliance in inpatient psychotherapy. *Psychotherapy Research*, *20*(2), 193–202.

Sennett, R. (2009). *The craftsman*. Yale University Press.

Shedler, J. (2010). The efficacy of psychodynamic psychotherapy. *American Psychologist*, *65*, 98–109.

Smith, D. (1991). *Hidden conversations: An introduction to communicative psychoanalysis*. Routledge.

Smith, D. (2018). *Hidden conversations: An introduction to communicative analysis*. New York.

Spengler, P. M., White, M. J., Ægisdóttir, S., Maugherman, A. S., Anderson, L. A., Cook, R. S., and Rush, J. D. (2009). The meta-analysis of clinical judgment project: Effects of experience on judgment accuracy. *The Counseling Psychologist*, *37*, 350–399. http://dx.doi.org/10.1177/0011000006295149

Strauss, B. M., and Petrowski, K. (2017). The role of the therapist's attachment in the process and outcome of psychotherapy. In L. G. Castonguay, and C. E. Hill (Eds.), *How and why are some therapists better than others? Understanding therapist effects* (p. 117–138). American Psychological Association. https://doi.org/10.1037/0000034-008

Sullivan, H. S. (1947). *Conceptions of modern psychiatry*. William A. White Psychiatric Foundation.

Sullivan, H. S. (1953). *The interpersonal theory of psychiatry*. Norton.

Tracey, T. J. G., Wampold, B. E., Lichtenberg, J. W., and Goodyear, R. K. (2014). Expertise in Psychotherapy: An Elusive Goal? *American Psychologist*, *69*, 218–229.

Tran, U., and Gregor, D. (2016). The relative efficacy of bona fide psychotherapies for post-traumatic stress disorder: A meta-analytical evaluation of randomized controlled trials. *BMC Psychiatry 16*, 266. https://doi.org/10.1186/s12888-016-0979-2

Truijens, F., Zulkevan Hulzen, L., and Vanheule, S. (2019). To manualize, or not to manualize: Is that still the question? A systematic review of empirical evidence for manual superiority in psychological treatment. *Journal of Clinical Psychology*, *75*(3), 329–343.

Tryon, G., Blackwell, S., and Hammel, E. (2007). A meta-analytic examination of client-therapist perspectives of the working alliance. *Psychotherapy Research*, *17*(6), 629–242.

Tryon, G., Birch, S., and Verkuilen, J. (2018). Meta-analyses of the relation of goal consensus and collaboration to psychotherapy outcome. *Psychotherapy*, *55*(4), 372.

Vacoch, D., and Strupp, H. (2000). The evolution of psychotherapy training: Reflections on manual-based learning and future alternatives. *Journal of Clinical Psychology*, *56*, 309–318.

Walfish, S., McAlister, B., O'Donnell, P., and Lambert, M. J. (2012). An investigation of self-assessment bias in mental health providers. *Psychological Reports, 110*(2), 639–644. https://doi.org/10.2466/02.07.17.PR0.110.2.2

Wampold, B. E. (2001). *The great psychotherapy debate*. Lawrence Erlbaum.

Wampold, B. E. (2007). *Qualities and actions of effective therapists*. American Psychological Association, Continuing Education Directorate.

Wampold, B. E. (2011). *Qualities and actions of effective psychotherapists. Video series I. Systems of psychotherapy*. American Psychological Associates.

Wampold, B. E. (2013). *The great psychotherapy debate* (revised ed.). Routledge.

Wampold, B. E. (2015). How important are the common factors in psychotherapy: An update. *World Psychiatry, 14*, 27–77.

Wampold, B., and Brown, J. (2006). Estimating variability in outcomes attributable to therapists: A naturalistic study of outcomes in managed care. *Journal of Consulting and Clinical Psychology, 73*(5), 920.

Wampold, B. E., and Budge, S. L. (2010). The 2011 Leona Tyler Award Address: The relationship—and its relationship to the common and specific factors of psychotherapy. *The Counseling Psychologist, 40*, 601–623.

Wampold, B., and Imel, Z. (2015). *The great psychotherapy debate: The evidence for what makes psychotherapy work*. Routledge.

Weinberger, J. (1995). Common factors are not so common: The common factors dilemma. *Clinical Psychology, 1*, 45–60.

Wayne, D., Butter, J., Siddall, V., Fudala, M., Wade, L., Feinglass, J., and McGaghie, W. (2006). Mastery learning of advanced cardiac life support skills by internal medicine residents using simulation technology and deliberate practice. *Journal of Internal Medicine, 21*(3), 251–256. doi.org/10.1111/j.1525-1497.2006.00341.x

Wiborg, I., and Dahl, A. (1996). Does brief dynamic psychotherapy reduce relapse rate of panic disorder? *Archives of General Psychiatry, 53*, 689–694.

Wierzbidki, M., and Pekorik, G. (1993). A meta-analysis of psychotherapy drop out. *Professional Psychology: Research and Practice, 24*, 190–195.

Wilcox, J., Raval, Z., Patel, A., Didwania, A., and Wayne, D. (2014). Imperfect beginnings: Incoming residents vary in their ability to interpret basic electrocardiogram findings. *Journal of Hospital Medicine, 9*, 197–198.

Index

A

alliance
    assessing common problems, 131–132
    building, 1–2, 7, 35
    insecure attachment and, 39–41
    moving from no alliance to, 73–76
    obstacles to developing, 64
    problem declaration and, 35
    strengthening, 120–123
    See also misalliance

ambivalence
    insecure attachments and, 99
    working with, 99–100

anxiety
    assessing, 16–19
    blocking strategy of ignoring, 23–32
    building capacity to pay attention to, 32–34
    depending and, 4, 61
    in parasympathetic nervous system, 16, 17, 18
    as pathway to healing, 4
    principle for high, 15
    in somatic nervous system, 16, 17, 18
    symptoms of, 16–19
    triggered by declaring problem, 15
    validating, 23
    will to do therapy and, 71–73
    See also anxiety regulation

anxiety regulation, 15–34
    blocking strategies that prevent, 23–32
    identifying anxiety symptoms and, 19–23
    necessity of, 1
    by paying attention to anxiety symptom, 23–32
    as work of therapist and patient together, 28

audio practicing, 11–12

avoidance strategies
    blocking, 23–32, 35, 42, 43, 46–47, 49, 50, 53, 55–57, 62
    frustration with, 52–53
    as pathway to healing, 4
    for problem declaration, 36–60
    turning, into positive goals, 106–107
    used by therapists, 95
    will to do therapy and, 62

C

capacities
    building, 109, 112
    lack of, 109–110

compassion
    being human and, 95
    self-, 127, 129

compliance, 62, 81–82

consensus, building, 112–114

D

defiance, deactivating, 62, 68–71, 83–85

denial
    dealing with, 7, 58–60, 96–97
    through fantasy, 89–93
    mirroring, 58
    through words, 93–95

depending
    anxiety and, 4, 61
    danger and, 4, 61
    invitation for, 35
    safety and, 15

desire to do therapy. *See* will to do therapy

discouragement, 129

dropouts from treatment
  behavior associated with, 119–120
  frequency of, 115
  identifying warning signs of, 115, 116–118
  predicting, 115
  preventing, 115–123

E
empathy
  being human and, 95
  simple vs. complex, 6, 93
expectations
  managing, 129
  turning negative, into realistic hope,
    110–112

F
fantasy, responding to denial through, 89–93
fears, addressing, 2
frustration, 52–53

G
goals. *See* positive goals

H
hope, realistic, from negative expectations,
    110–112
human, being, 95–96

I
insecure attachment
  ambivalence and, 99
  moving from, to secure attachment, 4
  problem declaration and, 36
  ruptures and, 115
  therapeutic relationship and, 3–4, 39–41
interrupting, 46–47

M
misalliance
  addressing and repairing, 120–123
  ambivalence and, 99
  behaviors, 119–120
  misperceptions and, 97
  sarcasm and, 102–103
  signs of, 116
misperceptions, identifying and deactivating,
    97–99

P
parasympathetic nervous system, anxiety in,
    16, 17, 18
passivity, addressing, 100–104
positive goals
  building consensus on, 112–114
  mobilizing patient to work toward, 104–114
  turning avoidance strategies into, 106–107
  turning lack of capacity into, 109–110
  turning negative goals into, 107–109
practice
  audio, 11–12
  common problems with, 127–129
  discouragement and, 129
  establishing habit of deliberate, 125–126
  expectation management and, 129
  finding time for, 127–128
  importance of, 9, 10–11
  monitoring, 126
  motivation and, 125, 128–129
  role-play, 11, 12–13
  self-compassion and, 127, 129
  self-criticism and, 127
problem declaration, 35–60
  avoidance strategies for, 36–60
  changing topics, 42–44
  insecure attachment and, 36
  therapeutic alliance and, 35
  vagueness and, 44–46

problems
    attributing to others, 49–51
    declaring, as trigger for excessive anxiety, 15
    denial of, 7, 58–60
    nonproblems vs. real, 36–39
    thoughts vs., 47–49
    turning, into positive goals, 104–105

R
reality, reminding patient of, 89–90
    See also denial
relational skills
    importance of, 1, 3, 9, 133
    lack of, by therapists, 9
    practicing, 9–13
repetition, importance of, for achieving mastery, 13
role-play practice, 11, 12–13
ruptures, healing, 120–123

S
safety
    co-creating, 15–34
    importance of, 15, 32
sarcasm, 102–103
secure attachment
    forming, with patients, 95–96
    moving from insecure attachment to, 4
    ruptures and, 115
self-compassion, 127, 129
self-criticism, 127
skill-building exercises
    guidelines for using, 10–13
    as progression, 11
    teacher's guide for using, 135–137
    See also relational skills
somatic nervous system, anxiety in, 16, 17, 18

T
therapeutic relationship
    importance of, 2–3, 7
    insecure attachment and, 3–4
    myths about, 5–7
    offering, 7
    resistance to, 6
    See also alliance
therapy, effective
    factors for, 1–3
    importance of clinical skills for, 9
    transtheoretical principles for, 131–132
    as work of therapist and patient together, 76, 80, 100–101
topics, changing, 42–44

V
vagueness, 44–46

W
will to do therapy
    anxiety and, 71–73
    attributing to others, 64–66, 76–80
    attributing to therapist, 66–68, 77, 85–87
    compliance and, 62, 81–82
    declaring, 61–76
    defiance and, 62, 68–71, 83–85
    as the engine of therapy, 64, 66, 68, 71, 80, 84, 86, 88, 131
    importance of, 61
    inviting, 62–64, 68
    mobilizing by using patient's words, 87–89
    mobilizing to work toward goal, 81–82
    myth about, 5–6
words, denial through, 93–95

About the Author

Jon Frederickson, MSW, is on the faculty of the Intensive Short-Term Dynamic Psychotherapy (ISTDP) Training Program at the Washington School of Psychiatry. He has been on the faculty of the Laboratorium Psykoeducaji in Warsaw and has taught at the Ersta Skondal Hogskole in Stockholm. Jon has provided ISTDP training in Sweden, Norway, Denmark, Poland, Italy, India, Iran, Australia, Canada, the United States, and the Netherlands. He is the author of over fifty published papers and four books, *Co-Creating Change: Effective Dynamic Therapy Techniques*; *Psychodynamic Psychotherapy: Learning to Listen from Multiple Perspectives*; *The Lies We Tell Ourselves: How to Face the Truth, Accept Yourself, and Create a Better Life*; and *Co-Creating Safety: Healing the Fragile Patient*. His book *Co-Creating Change* won first prize in psychiatry in 2014 at the British Medical Association Book Awards. It has been published in Farsi, Polish, and Slovak and is forthcoming in Spanish and Hebrew. *The Lies We Tell Ourselves* has been published in Polish, Farsi, Danish, Slovak, and Norwegian and is forthcoming in Arabic, German, Chinese, and Bulgarian.

Jon has DVDs of actual sessions with patients who previously failed in therapy at his websites www.istdpinstitute.com and www.deliberatepracticeinpsychotherapy.com. At these sites you will also find other skill-building exercises designed for therapists. Additionally, Jon answers therapists' questions on their work at www.facebook.com/DynamicPsychotherapy.